Urban Combat Service Support Operations
The Shoulders of Atlas

T0265218

Russell W. Glenn
Steven L. Hartman
Scott Gerwehr

Prepared for the United States Army

RAND
Arroyo Center

The research described in this report was sponsored by the United States Army under Contract No. DASW01-01-C-0003.

ISBN: 0-8330-3466-9

RAND is a nonprofit institution that helps improve policy and decisionmaking through research and analysis. RAND® is a registered trademark. RAND's publications do not necessarily reflect the opinions or policies of its research sponsors.

Cover artwork by Priscilla B. Glenn
Cover design by Barbara Caslon Angell

Published 2003 by RAND
1700 Main Street, P.O. Box 2138, Santa Monica, CA 90407-2138
1200 South Hayes Street, Arlington, VA 22202-5050
201 North Craig Street, Suite 202, Pittsburgh, PA 15213-1516
RAND URL: http://www.rand.org/
To order RAND documents or to obtain additional information, contact Distribution Services: Telephone: (310) 451-7002;
Fax: (310) 451-6915; Email: order@rand.org

The inevitability of U.S. armed forces future involvement in urban contingencies worldwide demands that those responsible for arming, manning, sustaining, and otherwise supporting these operations prepare for the challenges inherent in such undertakings. This report provides an overview of these formidable tasks and ways in which the U.S. Army combat service support (CSS) community can prepare itself to meet them. The analytical perspectives taken in the pages that follow include a macro overview as well as more focused investigations of specific functional areas.

This document will be of interest to individuals in the government and commercial sectors whose responsibilities include combat service support doctrine, policy design, funding, planning, preparation, or the development of technologies in support of civil or military operations in urban environments in both the immediate and longer-term future.

This research was sponsored by the U.S. Army's Combined Arms Support Command (CASCOM) and was conducted in the Force Development and Technology Program and the Military Logistics Program of RAND Arroyo Center. The Arroyo Center is a federally funded research and development center sponsored by the United States Army.

For more information on RAND Arroyo Center, contact the Director of Operations (telephone 310-393-0411, extension 6419; FAX 310-451-6952; e-mail Marcy_Agmon@rand.org), or visit the Arroyo Center's web site at http://www.rand.org/ard/.

CONTENTS

FIGURES

SUMMARY

That urban areas are among the most difficult of environments in which an army operates is historically established and widely recognized. Density explains much of the problem. In most other environments, those who fight on the ground have to concern themselves with a third dimension—the vertical—only in exceptional cases: when an enemy's aircraft threaten, when the adversary has learned to use a forest's trees as effective sniper hides, or when a mountainside provides concealment for the foe. The soldier or marine in a city, however, finds few times when height is not a concern as crucial as depth and width. There is more space to trouble a combatant; his potential problems are distributed over a volume rather than an area. Further, each layer of area within that volume potentially holds a greater density of threats. There are more enemy per unit of space and more friendly force personnel who can be accidentally killed or injured by comrades' fire. The many windows, doors, and other openings from places of concealment together comprise more possible firing positions. And there are more innocent civilians per unit volume, noncombatants whose lives should be spared if at all possible and whose presence therefore immeasurably complicates operations for everyone from the individual rifleman to the leaders managing thousands or tens of thousands of warriors. Many challenges exist even if the mission at hand does not involve combat. Buildings block radio signals, making it difficult to control subordinate unit efforts. Urban navigation is extraordinarily difficult, especially if a unit has only the standard scale military maps that lack the detail necessary to move about in a built-up area. The densely packed civilian population presents myriad mouths to feed or patients to support during humanitarian support efforts.

This closer packing of the consumers of the combat service support (CSS) soldier's services would seem to ease the logistical burden. Logic tells us that the distances between the points requiring support should be shorter. And so they often are, but instead of being dispersed only laterally, their separation is also vertical. Rather than two positions being linked by a short trench, they are separated by walls, buildings, several floors of a building, or a street under observation by an enemy awaiting a target. Two points disconnected by 150 meters in space could be apart by 30 minutes or more in travel time. Delivery of supplies and evacuation of the wounded is therefore lengthened and made more complicated. Transport times tend to be longer despite distances that appear short on a map. Quantities brought forward for distribution may have to be smaller due to the necessity of traveling along routes that traverse holes punched through building walls or the need to manhandle loads up stairwells, which translates to a greater number of trips to deliver the same quantity of supplies than would otherwise be the case.

The authors' previous analysis of the demands confronting a military force during urban operations and the CSS-specific research done in support of this study support the conclusion that CSS operations, like other ground force undertakings, need not undergo fundamental changes simply because the environment is urban. CSS personnel approaching urban tasks will instead be better served by for the most part employing tried-and-true doctrine while:

- Anticipating and adapting to environmental conditions.

- Recognizing that command and control requirements within CSS functional areas and between CSS, combat support, and combat elements should be uniform.

- Maintaining the flexibility essential to overcoming the extraordinary challenges inherent in urban undertakings.

ANTICIPATING AND ADAPTING TO ENVIRONMENTAL CONDITIONS

Developing and maintaining an organization's capability to anticipate and adapt during actions in densely populated areas will require considerable open-mindedness on the part of CSS leaders. On the one hand, the same decentralization of decisionmaking necessary in maneuver and combat support units is essential for effective provision of logistical and other services. Drivers, medics, and other junior personnel will be those CSS personnel closest to the action. It is they who should be trained to constantly monitor the tactical situation, for conditions often change dramatically during urban operations and these individuals will be in a position to first notice these changes. The same soldiers need to know how to react when the situation is fundamentally altered: how to best continue pursuit of task accomplishment, to whom they should report information of intelligence value, and how to respond when communications fail.

Yet though leaders will most likely adapt by accepting greater decentralization in decisionmaking, the limited availability of many CSS assets will encourage centralized management of these often too-scarce resources. The same structures that interfere with radio communications and global positioning system (GPS) signals separate units from each other. A platoon medic will find himself unable to aid a casualty two squads away; those calling for his assistance will find that rapidly locating or communicating with him may be impossible. Commanders will therefore have to consider heavily weighting front-line units with such low-density capabilities or keeping the assets centrally located in the immediate rear area for dispatch when needed. Habitual CSS task organization relationships and table of organization and equipment (TOE) allocations are likely to prove inadequate to the demands of future urban missions.

RECOGNIZING THAT COMMAND AND CONTROL REQUIREMENTS WITHIN CSS FUNCTIONAL AREAS AND BETWEEN CSS, COMBAT SUPPORT, AND COMBAT ELEMENTS SHOULD BE UNIFORM

Adjustments will be similarly demanded of those responsible for command, control, and communications (C^3). CSS resources will in most cases require the same radio capabilities, maps or overhead imagery, and intelligence feeds as do other types of units. The porous nature of the urban environment means that even the rear-most areas are vulnerable to attacks by infiltrators or disgruntled civilians. The safety of CSS soldiers as well as their ability to provide adequate support will demand that their leaders have the same level of situational awareness that has become the norm for soldiers at the line of contact. There is positive payback for the expenditures inherent in better equipping the men and women providing support. As noted, the responsibilities of fuel transporters, drivers, maintenance personnel, chaplains, and many others cause them to travel throughout an area of operations. These individuals are a potentially vital source of intelligence during any type of operation. Properly trained and equipped with the means to determine their location and report what is seen, each such soldier should be viewed as an intelligence-collection asset. CSS C^3 responsibilities can include far more complex requirements as well. It might be appropriate, for example, to assign overall responsibility for an operation to a CSS officer if the primary objectives involve support operations, e.g., during a humanitarian relief undertaking.

MAINTAINING THE FLEXIBILITY ESSENTIAL TO OVERCOMING THE EXTRAORDINARY CHALLENGES INHERENT IN URBAN UNDERTAKINGS

An urban environment confronts CSS soldiers with many other extraordinary challenges. Personnel attrition and some materiel consumption rates tend to be higher than in other environments (though few reliable planning factors exist in this regard). Historically, men have too often been killed or wounded in appalling numbers during urban battles. Ammunition, vehicle, and other consumption rates can exceed several times over that found in combat elsewhere. Demands on suppliers will be exceptional even during operations in which combat plays no role. The density of noncombatants requiring support means that transportation, medical, and other unit types can be overwhelmed. It might be advisable to work intimately with coalition nation and private enterprises attempting to achieve similar objectives, dividing functional responsibilities and relying on each other for given capabilities.

CONCLUDING OBSERVATIONS

CSS considerations relevant to the three factors noted above receive an expanded consideration in each chapter of the report. The appendix contains a list of over one hundred observations and recommendations extracted from the main body text for ease of reference. The U.S. Army's combat service support community is currently capable of meeting the most likely mission requirements inherent in operations encompassing hamlets, villages, and small towns. Barring the incidence of combat, it may similarly be able to accomplish assigned support and stability operation-related tasks in larger towns and even small cities should the level of noncombatant support demanded not be overly great. The same is not true should sustained and intense combat play an eminent role during such undertakings or should the area of concern be a major city whose citizens need a significant level of support. The rocket-propelled grenades and small arms fire ubiquitous during most urban combat actions pose lethal threats to support personnel in virtually every CSS vehicle type. There currently exists no means of adequately protecting crews and passengers from these threats, or from the mines so frequently found in built-up areas. Urban planning factors that would help in determining likely personnel replacement rates and class of supply consumption do not exist even in the most basic form. Doctrine needed to guide such planning and other preparations, to include training, virtually ignores CSS urban operations demands. The CSS community is by no means alone. The situation is little better for most components of combat and combat support operations.

The news is not entirely negative, however. As alluded to above, there is no reason to believe that the same doctrine that guides the Army's preparation for peacetime and war actions elsewhere cannot also serve as the foundation for urban undertakings. Similarly, the skills taught during training conducted in other environments holds many lessons for the soldier awaiting commitment to action in a city, town, or smaller built-up area. Service leaders can adapt rather than have to start anew when preparing doctrine, developing training, and otherwise propelling the Army toward an acceptable level of urban preparedness. Though equipment is deficient, sometimes seriously deficient, in its suitability for urban contingencies, the overall quality of those systems and the soldiers that employ them virtually guarantees eventual tactical success during even the most strenuous of operations. But the length of time needed to achieve that success and the number of American casualties suffered will be greater than would otherwise be the case until improvements are made. The gap between existent and potential levels of readiness could be the difference between strategic success and failure.

This analysis does not claim to be comprehensive despite the scope of research and breadth of results. It is merely an introduction, an initial attempt to help move the U.S. Army toward a greater CSS competence to undertake operations in an environment that has become a routine component of any deployment. Each of the many components that together comprise the whole—maintenance and transportation, medical and supply, personnel management and arming, and others equally critical to success—warrant closer scrutiny in determining where they are and what needs to be done so that America's soldiers are prepared for tomorrow's worldwide security challenges.

ACKNOWLEDGMENTS

The authors would first and foremost like to thank Tom Edwards and the many other representatives of the U.S. Army Combined Arms Support Command (CASCOM) for their extraordinary interest and support as sponsors of the work that follows. The topic is one that has long been in need of analysis; it is to these many ladies and gentlemen that credit for this initial step is due. Major Ben Roth of the Canadian Army and the U.S. Army's Captain Sean F. Del Grego provided vital and most appreciated review comments. Major Kevin Born was extraordinary in his role as CASCOM's primary point of contact. This fine officer's early review did much to enhance the study's value for those in the field. The authors also acknowledge the support of Mr. Albert H. Pomey, Doctrine Division of the U.S. Army Armor School, whose expertise on the M908 Multi-purpose, Anti-Tank (MPAT) round significantly improved the information provided in this report.

There are a considerable number of individuals whose interviews and suggestions during telephone calls or face-to-face discussions resulted in important insights on one or more areas of pertinence to this study. These many individuals are recognized in footnotes and the bibliography where possible. We extend our thanks to them and any others whose help might not be so noted but whose kindness in taking the time to assist is nonetheless most appreciated.

Matthew Lewis and John Halliday provided very beneficial reviews of the final draft, efforts for which the authors are thankful. Becky Bower and Terri Perkins are responsible for the formatting and much more in the way of administrative help in creating this document.

Nikki Shacklett's editing was once again nothing short of superb. Our gratitude, ladies, for your consistently outstanding work.

ABBREVIATIONS

A&L	Administration and Logistics
AAFARS	Advance Aviation Forward Area Refueling System
AFB	Air Force Base
AGU	Airborne Guidance Unit
AHS	Assault Hoseline System
AO	Area of Operations
APC	Armored Personnel Carrier
ARVN	Army of the Republic of Vietnam
ASEAN	Association of Southeast Asian Nations
ATTN	Attention
BDAR	Battle Damage Assessment and Repair
BSB	Brigade Support Battalion
C-DAY	Mobilization Day
C^3	Command, Control, and Communications
C4ISR	Command, Control, Communications, Computers, Intelligence, Surveillance, and Reconnaissance
CA	Civil Affairs
CALL	U.S. Army Center for Army Lessons Learned

CASCOM	Combined Arms Support Command
CCIR	Commander's Critical Information Requirements
CDR	Commander
CEP	Circular Error Probable
CIWP	Canteen Insert Water Purifier
CMOC	Civil-Military Operations Center
COA	Course of Action
COTS	Commercial Off-the-Shelf
CRT	Combat Repair Team
CS	Combat Support
CSH	Combat Support Hospital
CSS	Combat Service Support
CSSC	Combat Service Support Company
DISCOM	Division Support Command
DLA	Defense Logistics Agency
DMC	Distribution Management Center
DMFD	D-Day Mobile Fuel Distribution System
DSA	Division Support Area
DZ	Drop Zone
EAB	Echelons Above Brigade
EOD	Explosive Ordnance Disposal
EPW	Enemy Prisoners of War
FALANTIL	East Timor's Pro-Independence Militia Organization
FBCB2	Force XXI Battle Command, Brigade and Below
FCS	Future Combat System
FLE	Forward Logistics Element

FM	Field Manual
FMC	Forward Maintenance Company
FSB	Forward Support Battalion
GPH	Gallons Per Hour
GPM	Gallons Per Minute
GPS	Global Positioning System
HEMTT	Heavy Expanded Mobility Tactical Truck
HMMWV	High-Mobility Multi-Purpose Wheeled Vehicle
HN	Host Nation
HQ	Headquarters
HUMINT	Human Intelligence
IO	Information Operations
IPB	Intelligence Preparation of the Battlefield
ISB	Intermediate Support Base
IV	Intravenous
JP	Joint Publication
JTF	Joint Task Force
JUO	Joint Urban Operation
LAV	Light Amphibious Vehicle
LCAC	Landing Craft Air Cushion
LHS	Load Handling System
LMFF	Load Handling System Modular Fuel Farm
LMSR	Large Medium-Speed Roll-On/Roll-Off Ships
LN	Local National
LOGPAC	Logistics Package
LOS	Line-of-Sight
LWP	Light Water Purifier

LZ	Landing Zone
MAGTF	USMC Marine Air/Ground Task Force
MAO	Mortuary Affairs Officer
MCL	Mission Configured Load
MCWL	Marine Corps Warfighting Laboratory
MD	Medical Doctor
MEDEVAC	Medical Evacuation
MEMS	Micro-Electrical Mechanical System
METT-TC	Mission, Enemy, Terrain and weather, Troops and support available, Time available, and Civilian considerations
MG	Major General
MOOTW	Military Operations Other Than War
MOS	Military Occupational Specialty
MOUT	Military Operations on Urbanized Terrain
MPAT	Multi-purpose, Anti-Tank
MRE	Meals Ready to Eat
MSR	Main Supply Route
MTOE	Mission Table of Organization and Equipment
NATO	North Atlantic Treaty Organization
NGO	Nongovernmental Organization
NLEC	Nonlethal Effects Cell
OEM	Original Equipment Manufacturer
OPSEC	Operations Security
ORF	Operational Readiness Float
PA	Physician's Assistant
PEGASYS	Precision, Extended Glide, and Air Drop System

PIR	Priority Intelligence Requirements
PLL	Prescribed Load List
PLS	Palletized Load System
POL	Petroleum, Oil, and Lubricant
PSYOP	Psychological Operations
PVO	Private Volunteer Organization(s)
QRF	Quick Reaction Force
RIFTS	Rapidly Installed Fuel Transfer System
ROE	Rules of Engagement
ROWPU	Reverse Osmosis Water Purification Unit
RPG	Rocket-Propelled Grenade
RSTA	Reconnaissance, Surveillance, and Target Acquisition
RTF	Ready-to-Fight
SAMS	Standard Army Maintenance System
SBCT	Stryker Brigade Combat Team
SCL	Strategic Configured Load
SES	Surface Effect Ship
SITREP	Situation Report
SOP	Standard Operating Procedure
SPOD	Sea Point of Debarkation
SRC	Standard Requirement Code
SSA	Supply Support Activity
SSG	Staff Sergeant
STONS	Short Tons
TARDEC	Tank Automotive Research, Development, and Engineering Center

TNDS	Transdermal Nutrient Delivery System
TOC	Tactical Operations Center
TOE	Table of Organization and Equipment
TRADOC	Training and Doctrine Command
TSV	Theater Support Vessel
TTP	Tactics, Techniques, and Procedures
TWPS	Tactical Water Purification System
UAV	Unmanned Aerial Vehicle
UCL	Unit Configured Load
UCLA	University of Southern California, Los Angeles
UGV	Unmanned Ground Vehicle
UN	United Nations
UO	Urban Operations
UPS	Uninterruptible Power Supply
USMC	United States Marine Corps
WMD	Weapons of Mass Destruction

INTRODUCTION

> The soldier cannot be a fighter and a pack animal at one and the same time, any more than a field piece can be a gun and a supply vehicle combined.
>
> J.F.C. Fuller, c. 1948

Today's men and women serving in combat service support (CSS) units are akin to the ancient warrior Atlas. The mythological Greek was a god of tremendous strength tasked with the burden of bearing the heavens and sky, much as it is the duty of today's CSS soldiers to support military operations worldwide.[1] The similarity to the warrior Atlas is heightened when these men and women are committed to urban operations. Their skills as fighters are likely to be tested no less than their ability to shoulder their martial loads, burdens that will at times include supporting not only a U.S. force but also coalition members, noncombatant civilians, and possibly even members of private volunteer and nongovernmental organizations (PVOs and NGOs). It is conceivable, perhaps even desirable, that a CSS officer will be tasked to lead an American force if its primary mission is to support a local civilian population.

Urban CSS operations are in many ways business as usual, relying on the same fundamentals of doctrine and training as for virtually any other mission. But there is also a considerable likelihood that these operations will present transporters, quartermasters, medics, and

---

[1]Robert Graves, *The Greek Myths, Volume One,* Baltimore: Penguin, 1968, pp. 143–146.

their brethren with challenges greater in scope and magnitude than are confronted elsewhere. It is the purpose of this report to identify the nature of these challenges and propose approaches for overcoming them.

The authors' primary chronological focus is the next ten years, the decade encompassing the period from the present to the pending fielding of the U.S. Army's Objective Force. The need to confront the problems associated with urban CSS operations during this period is an essential one. America's soldiers already find themselves in urban areas during virtually every operation they undertake. Their tools— doctrine, training, technology, and force structure—are not always up to the demands those undertakings make on them. Like their comrades manning combat and combat support units, those who provide combat service support during an urban operation have yet to fully prepare for its many and varied formidable tasks.

What follows is an initial identification and consideration of these challenges. The opening chapters take a macro perspective that encompasses CSS responsibilities writ large. Thereafter, the many functional areas that together comprise the U.S. Army's combat service support force structure receive individual attention. Together the general and specific considerations provide an introduction to the challenges inherent in supporting military operations in built-up areas and ways to overcome these challenges. This is a first look at a topic overdue for analysis, and our objective is to establish a foundation for building urban operations readiness in the immediate and longer terms.

The reader will find passages that employ a particular system or force structure as exemplars. The specific vehicle or unit type is less important than the general vulnerabilities or capabilities it represents. The objective is to abet understanding in the service of finding solutions, regardless of the organization to which a soldier, sailor, marine, or airman belongs.

Chapter Two

THE NATURE OF THE BURDEN: THE CHALLENGES URBAN OPERATIONS BRING TO BEAR

Focus attacks on service support and unprotected soldiers . . . . Urban operations are characterized by the isolation of small groups and navigational challenges; the separation it creates enables the enemy to inflict maximum casualties even when there is no other direct military benefit from this action.

Fighting in Built-Up Areas

Villages, towns, and cities present a greater density of challenges for military men and women than any other battlefield or any other area of operations. There are more friendly forces in smaller volumes of terrain—and volume is the appropriate measure, for urban operations by nature include surface, below-ground, and above-ground components. There are greater numbers of noncombatants in less space. There are larger numbers of buildings, roads, potential barriers, and possible enemy firing positions in the built-up area. And there may be more enemies packed into those spaces, waiting behind those barriers, and occupying those weapon positions. The consequences are considerable for both defender and attacker. Instead of deploying soldiers in one defensive position to cover several square kilometers of terrain, a defender finds that a city street offers oversight only along its own narrow corridor. Many other possible enemy approaches exist within a few city blocks, each possibly needing its own defensive position if it is to be monitored. The result is that a maneuver commander requires more positions, closer to each other, either to defend against attacks or to attack along the many mobility corridors or through buildings. The distances between his and other friendly units are less than on other ground. He is likely to find that the offset separating those units and the enemy is similarly less.

The result is an unfortunate dichotomy for the CSS warrior. Greater friendly force density would appear to make the providers' tasks easier. Logic would seem to dictate that more supported units in less space would translate to less distance between a similar number of nodes than would be found on more open terrain. But the service supporter frequently finds the opposite to be the case. There may be more units in a given volume, but one position is often not directly accessible from another because of enemy fires or physical barriers. Members even of such lower-echelon units as squads and platoons are dispersed and not within sight of each other. Instead of a squad's members lying together within a tree line, two men peer from a basement window, three others from a second-floor balcony, and another pair from a pile of rubble down the street. A machine gun team observes its field of fire through a rooftop hole. In open farm-land, a tank platoon assigned to support a light infantry company tends to maintain its unit integrity, all vehicles working together. In a city, those systems are likely to be allocated singly or in pairs, the better to support the squads or platoons that are typically the eche-lon conducting tactical urban operations. Thus the dichotomy: ele-ments requiring support are consolidated in a smaller space, while the nodes to which the CSS warrior must provide support are greater in number and take longer to move between than on other terrain. The straight-line distances between them might be less than in a desert or pasture, but the convoluted route necessary to reach each safely without compromising those who seek to avoid enemy eyes makes the actual distance far greater. Providing timely support will thus be harder and CSS resources will be stretched thinner.

The density of structures on urban terrain will challenge CSS leaders in other ways as well. Some support units, maintenance companies for example, require very large areas to perform their missions. Such units can easily occupy a square kilometer of open ground even without other units' vehicles present for repair or servicing. As buildings occupy much of what would be open space, organizations like this will most likely have to spread themselves over a much larger area than would otherwise be the norm (with consequent costs for command, control, and security). Alternatively, the unit can compress itself into an available space, thereby increasing congestion and making itself a more densely packed and lucrative target.

The phenomenon of increased densities further directly influences the following additional factors of particular importance during CSS operations in urban areas, each of which is discussed in greater detail below:

- Force security and noncombatant safety

- Scope of CSS operational responsibilities

- Number and type of civil authority echelons that can affect military operations

- Increased difficulty of navigation

- Higher consumption rates

- Greater reliance on human intelligence

FORCE SECURITY AND NONCOMBATANT SAFETY

Heavily populated built-up areas pose dramatic force protection challenges for the CSS soldier. The aforementioned higher density of potential approach routes—whether streets, alleys, subterranean passageways, or building floors above ground—means that enemy infiltration behind friendly forward units can be virtually impossible to detect much less interdict. Every CSS headquarters, convoy, and other node (mobile or static) therefore needs to maintain constant alertness and a capability to defend itself. Vehicles such as fuel tankers and ammunition trucks are particularly lucrative, as they give an urban attack more "bang for the buck" than many other targets due to their lack of armor protection, impact on actions at the line of contact, and explosive contents. Bulking up convoy security with engineers, military police, aviation support, and other means may be called for. Nevertheless, convoy security is complicated by the considerable number of potential weapon positions and ubiquitous presence of individuals in civilian clothing (most of whom are civilians, though some are enemy attired as if they were). The challenge is particularly acute for combat service providers because of the duration and frequency of their exposure. They have to traverse miles of urban streets and can be committed to providing support to the indigenous population at locations far from the relative safety of base camps. The oft-times complicated nature of urban politics makes even humanitarian missions risky if the support being rendered threatens the preeminence of one or more factions. Combat service support leaders will have to exercise care as they seek to select locations that both serve the primary task and allow those executing it to protect themselves. Again, every deployment should be capable of self-defense. It should also incorporate well-planned, coordinated, and rehearsed plans for reinforcement and withdrawal, each of which has multiple contingency plans that address routes to be used and types of fire support available, and are flexible enough to cope with situations that could range from civilian riots to all-out enemy assault.

Site selection, the choice of convoy routes, and other decisions should also take into account the possibility of an enemy attack with weapons of mass destruction (WMD), should the foe have such a capability. The precautions taken will depend on the nature of those capabilities. For example, alternatives to locating medical aid facilities in basements or other low-lying areas might be desirable if a chemical threat is a major concern, since some hazardous agents are heavier than air and thus tend to settle in low-lying areas. Potential decontamination sites should likewise be identified and prepared for use even if the requisite equipment is not prepositioned.

Leaders should designate alternative routes during convoy planning in case obstacles, demonstrations, a change in the enemy situation, or contamination block original routes. Such contamination could be the result of WMD use or an accident involving industrial, medical, or other hazardous wastes frequently found in built-up areas. It may fall to CSS units to assist in the cleanup or removal of such hazardous wastes (or WMD munitions) upon their discovery and to provide aid to those suffering exposure.

It would seem that a typical town or city would have a large number of routes available for CSS use. In reality the actual number is significantly reduced by myriad operational considerations. These include:

• Obstacles along some traveled ways

- The dangers posed to indigenous personnel by military vehicles and the consequent desire to use routes through less populated areas

- The condition of road surfaces

- Height and width restrictions

- The volume of civilian or other military traffic

- Threats from armed personnel or mobs

Indigenous residents may covet even such waste as discarded mess hall food or scrap metal, making it necessary to vary procedures, routes, and times of operation so as to minimize threats to friendly force personnel and reduce the chances of inadvertently injuring civilians. Aircraft may be the preferable means of transport to minimize such risks if surface-to-air threat levels, the nature of the task at hand, and other demands on aviation assets make their use feasible.

Urban noncombatant density spawns several additional security issues. Unlike in most open areas, large numbers of noncombatants will be in virtually constant contact with friendly forces. Theft from stationary storage locations, distribution points, and even moving vehicles will be a consistent threat. Rules of engagement (ROE) and guidance on the use of available weapons (perhaps including non-lethal capabilities) should be clearly articulated and rehearsed to preclude unfortunate overreactions or unnecessary endangerment of U.S. lives.

The ceaseless proximity of noncombatants further ordains that a military force's actions will be under perpetual observation. The ubiquity of civilian eyes means that interested parties will have access to constant updates on friendly force dispositions and, potentially, the intentions of that force. Locals will quickly discern patterns of behavior, habits, and an organization's vulnerabilities. Deception and rigorous operations security (OPSEC) procedures will both have roles to play. The greatest threat to force security can be a complacency born of routine. CSS elements will repeatedly deploy throughout an operational area during virtually any operation. Units may go weeks or months without significant threat contact. Such cases will cause security standards to slip in all but the most disciplined of units. Even otherwise disciplined soldiers will adopt shortcuts as routine (e.g., repeatedly using the quickest travel routes or failing to wear helmet and protective armor) rather than consciously and continuously varying their procedures unless leaders enforce stringent standards.[1]

SCOPE OF CSS OPERATIONAL RESPONSIBILITIES

CSS operations conducted within urban environs are unlikely to relieve a commander and his soldiers of any of the responsibilities they would have on other terrain. They are, however, quite likely to entail additional duties and an expansion of traditional taskings, both of which are directly attributable to the greater density of individuals found in villages, towns, or cities as compared to other environments.

In general, CSS organizations are manned and equipped to support the U.S. forces with which they are deployed. Urban contingencies will not alter this fundamental relationship. They will, however, tend to complicate it. Such challenges include:

- Longer transport of water (many parts of cities become deserts if public water supplies are cut off).

- The collection, storage, and destruction of threat munitions and weapons in considerable quantities.

- Provision of support and the construction of containment facilities for large numbers of enemy prisoners of war (EPW), detainees, and displaced persons.

- Evacuation and treatment of greater numbers of U.S. casualties. Casualties during urban combat are historically higher than in other environments. Moving and treating wounded can also pose extraordinary difficulties. Evacuation requirements can include bringing wounded down from upper floors of buildings,

---

[1]An excellent example of the dangers inherent in complacency is evident in "Witness the Evil." This Canadian Forces Production video portrays a soldier at risk when he is stopped by threatening indigenous personnel while driving. The man, traveling alone with a single vehicle along a familiar and repeatedly used route, finds himself without reinforcement or a means to communicate his plight when he is suddenly confronted by aggressive locals. See "Witness the Evil," Canadian Forces Production videotape, Ottawa: DGPA-National Defense Headquarters, Cat. #31-0898F, undated.

navigating through undersized "mouse holes" blown in walls, and taking other convoluted routes so as to minimize the amount of fire to which medics and their charges are exposed.

- Potentially increased rates of stress-induced combat exhaustion.

- Extraordinary physical exertion that necessitates more frequent rotation of forces (there is evidence that rotation also has the benefit of mitigating the number of stress casualties).

- Increased vulnerability of utility aircraft to ground fires.

- Provision of support to friendly special operations forces working with or in close proximity to regular units.

As the discussion below will reflect, this list is by no means exhaustive.

The scope of CSS responsibilities may also include support of coalition members, representatives of nongovernmental organizations and private volunteer organizations (NGOs and PVOs), and commercial enterprises in addition to that provided to indigenous noncombatants and captured enemy. Recent multinational operations involving U.S. forces have at times included representatives from nations unable to fully support their deployed forces. Calls by coalition members for U.S. support have in other instances been due less to an inability to provide assistance than to a desire to take advantage of superior U.S. capabilities (e.g., medical care). Urban operations put coalition forces in closer proximity to each other. The number of such requests is therefore likely to be greater during such contingencies. Operational readiness or coalition politics may dictate that they be granted despite the resultant burden on U.S. CSS units. U.S. Marine Corps forces found themselves providing various types of assistance to members of the media during their 2002 operations in and around Kandahar, Afghanistan. Already tasked with requirements beyond those initially expected, scarce resources were further stretched by having to support fifty members of these various commercial organizations.[2] Similarly, NGO and PVO representatives may come to U.S. forces for assistance otherwise not available in a

---

[2]Russell W. Glenn interview with 5th Special Forces Group representatives, September 19, 2002, Tampa, Florida.

theater. During Operation Restore Hope in Somalia during 1992 and 1993, for example, nongovernmental organizations were unable to provide adequate security to prevent the loss of medicines and food to thieves. Military personnel were asked to provide the security needed.[3]

Friendly force medical capabilities can also be strained by having to treat the large numbers of enemy wounded that can characterize urban conflict. Combined with the expected increases in U.S. and noncombatant wounded, medical personnel could find themselves overwhelmed and short of supplies imported and maintained at stock levels established based on experiences in less casualty-intensive environments. Civil-Military Operations Centers (CMOC) are used to coordinate supporting efforts involving PVOs, NGOs, and noncombatants, but the extent of demand during operations in urban areas may require that they be augmented by CSS experts to aid in planning and managing available assets.[4] Coordination with CSS headquarters will in any case be essential to ensure effective synchronization of military and civilian support activities.

It is very likely that in a built-up area, the greatest expansion of CSS urban responsibilities will involve the protection and care of local noncombatants. Such care will be the driving force behind some deployments. Such was the case during the 1990s in Haiti and in the opening months of operations in Somalia. It is hoped that a military force so tasked would be manned, equipped, and provisioned to meet the demands of both military and civilian care in such instances. In other scenarios, however, assistance to the indigenous population is supplemental to the primary mission of supporting the American fighting force. Paris in 1944 provides a historical example. General Eisenhower made it known that bypassing the French capital was desirable from the perspective of sustaining the allied offen-

---

[3]Elspeth C. Ritchie and Robert Mott, "Caring for Civilians During Peace Keeping Missions: Priorities and Decisions," *Military Medicine* 167 (Supplement 3, 2002), p. 14.

[4]"The mission of the CMOC is to coordinate the military and civilian aspects of the humanitarian assistance effort by providing the linkage between the military commander and other governmental agencies and nongovernmental organizations (NGOs)." Clay Cooper, "Military Operations Center (CMOC)," Fort Leavenworth, KS: Center for Army Lessons Learned News from the Front," January–February 1997, *http://call.army.mil/products/nftf/janfeb97/civmil.htm*, accessed October 16, 2002.

sive. Seizing Paris would task his force with the support of tens of thousands of civilians, each needing food, water, fuel, and other essentials. Eisenhower was nevertheless ordered to capture the city. Political decisions resulted in civilian assistance taking *de facto* precedence over combat operations. A future military force so tasked will be hard pressed if not stretched beyond its capacity to address both its traditional and indigenous population–related requirements.

NUMBER AND TYPE OF CIVIL AUTHORITY ECHELONS THAT CAN AFFECT MILITARY OPERATIONS

The greater numbers of human beings and more physical infrastructure found in urban areas translate to more demands on military authorities to govern and maintain the two during operations. Military leaders might therefore find themselves having to coordinate with neighborhood, city, and regional representatives in addition to those at national level. These various echelons can be notably heterogeneous in their motivations and methods of operating. City government officials may include those from the mayor's office, urban council, police and fire departments, and many others. Failure to consider the implications of the presence of many varied interests can have immediate operational consequences. Senior commanders ought to assign areas of operation (AOs) that facilitate rather than hinder subordinates' coordination with these entities. For example, during the California Army National Guard's support of the City of Los Angeles during its 1992 riots, military commanders assigned AOs based on easily identified terrain features such as major highways, a practice in keeping with standard military practice. They later found that they could have drawn unit boundaries in a manner that considerably reduced the number of precincts and fire stations with which subordinate unit commanders had to maintain liaison, had the higher headquarters first coordinated with local authorities.[5]

---

[5]For more on military operations during this domestic contingency, see James Delk, "MOUT: A Domestic Case Study—The 1992 Los Angeles Riots," in Russell W. Glenn et al. (eds.), *The City's Many Faces: Proceedings of the RAND Arroyo-MCWL-J8 UWG Urban Operations Conference,* Santa Monica, CA: RAND, 2000, pp. 79–157.

They are often not a formal part of urban governments, but a city's influential clan, family, tribe, trade union, or commercial enterprises can prove very beneficial in helping to meet operational requirements. Establishing cordial relationships with these as well as the previously mentioned official authorities can considerably abet good military-civilian relations during a force's presence in a given urban area. Such favorable relations pay dividends when the inevitable misunderstandings or points of disagreement later arise, as well as facilitating intelligence collection.

INCREASED DIFFICULTY OF NAVIGATION

Virtually every urban surface has the potential to influence radio or global positioning system (GPS) transmissions in some way. Urban command and control will consequently be complicated. CSS leaders must be prepared for frequent breaks in contact with higher and subordinate elements. Plans will have to incorporate means of handling such lapses. Disruption of GPS signals leaves traditional land navigation skills as the backup. Unfortunately, cities and towns are notoriously difficult terrain in which to navigate. Structures can reduce line of sight to tens of meters, if that. Road signs, if they exist at all, are often removed or deliberately altered to confuse non-natives. The refuse of war can turn one-time landmarks into unrecognizable rubble. Innovation becomes the norm. A burned-out hulk, animal carcass, or other feature becomes a checkpoint. Leaders have to ensure that those in charge of units are trained to assume the greater responsibilities that come from operating without consistent communications. The CSS warrior has to adapt his movement techniques and security procedures to account for navigation difficulties. Having to reverse the direction of travel for a convoy that includes oversized vehicles can endanger both military and indigenous personnel. Repeated use of previously identified routes offers the observant enemy opportunities for ambush. Preliminary route reconnaissance by ground elements is often not feasible in high-threat environments. (If the assets are available, this constraint can be overcome via the use of manned or unmanned overhead reconnaissance systems.) Circumventing the built-up area to the extent possible and reentering it only when necessary can further reduce exposure. On-the-spot innovation will be in constant demand of even individual vehicle commanders.

Night operations will be as desirable as they are in other environments, but darkness only further complicates movement problems. Navigation during periods of limited visibility will be a considerable challenge. In addition to the lack of visibility compounding the difficulties already noted, ambient light sources such as fires, security or street lighting, and advertising can interfere with night-vision devices worn by those both on the ground and in the air.

Maps seldom show the desired level of resolution necessary for urban military operations. Desirable scales (generally 1:12,500 or larger) are not a military standard, but smaller scales fail to show individual structures, streets, or the detail needed to successfully plan and conduct tactical activities. A six-digit grid coordinate provides 100-meter accuracy, generally adequate for controlling artillery fires in the open. In a city, an "on target" round relying on that same accuracy could land a block away from its objective, striking noncombatants or friendly forces instead. The individual attempting to adjust the fire might not even be able to see the round land due to limited lines of sight.[6] Similarly, such inherent error is sufficient to cause mechanics to bypass a disabled vehicle, a convoy to miss its destination, or a medic to miss recovering a wounded soldier or marine, especially if the latter is concealed within a structure.

Navigation, command, and control are further complicated by language problems. Various spellings for an identical street or other terrain feature can differ from map to map, sign to sign, or in briefings and orders from various headquarters. The systems used to transliterate certain languages (e.g., Arabic and Chinese) to Anglicized alphabets often result in names being spelled in several, frequently considerably different ways.[7] The 10th Mountain Division's

---

[6]This was a problem for infantry commanders leading Israeli units during 1973 fighting in downtown Suez City, Egypt. BG (IDF, ret.) Nachum Zaken, Battalion Commander, 433 Armored Battalion, Armored Brigade #500 during 1973 fighting in Suez City, interview with Russell W. Glenn, Latrun, Israel, April 10, 2000.

[7]Perhaps the best, and certainly the most interesting, description of this condition as it applies to Arabic appears in T.E. Lawrence's *Seven Pillars of Wisdom:* "Arabic names won't go into English, exactly, for their consonants are not the same as ours, and their vowels, like ours, vary from district to district. There are some 'scientific systems' of transliteration, helpful to people who know enough Arabic not to need helping, but a washout for the world. I spell my names anyhow, to show what rot the systems are." T. E. Lawrence, *Seven Pillars of Wisdom,* New York: Doubleday, 1965, p. 25.

Division Support Command (DISCOM) designated standard spellings for features during their operations in Somalia, thereby ensuring that at least their internal communications were consistent. Even with such initiative, however, drivers and others will have to compensate for varied spellings on street signs or other civilian signage.

HIGHER CONSUMPTION RATES

The high consumption rates that have historically characterized military urban operations will obviously have direct impact on CSS providers. Manpower losses, whether due to wounds, fatalities, disease and other nonbattle injury, or combat stress reaction, will task medical, mortuary affairs, and adjutant general assets. Selected Class V (ammunition) consumption significantly exceeds norms found on other terrain, though here as in the case of manpower losses there are no planning factors available that account specifically for urban contingencies. Increased wear and tear will result in a greater number of requests for boots, uniforms, tires, and other items of equipment that suffer from constant contact with the abrasive surfaces that characterize urban terrain. Similarly, personnel will both request and wear out gloves, knee and elbow pads, and selected weapons parts in greater numbers due to hard-surface impacts.

GREATER RELIANCE ON HUMAN INTELLIGENCE

Walls, roofs, and other structural features interrupt line-of-sight (LOS) and make overhead imagery of less value in urban areas than in others. Such barriers preclude penetration by even infrared or other capabilities that are able to "see" through foliage and similar concealment in other than man-made environments. What is in the open or under visible camouflage nets elsewhere is completely hidden within structures during urban contingencies. Further, movement of units is less frequently evident. Well-trained organizations minimize exterior activities; their soldiers remain within buildings to the maximum extent possible to reduce detection. Vehicles leave few signs of their passage on asphalt and concrete, unlike in other areas where their tracks can be seen in dirt or compressed foliage. The same LOS obstacles that interfere with friendly force communications block signal-collection efforts. The city foe will in some instances employ local telephone systems, cellular networks, or other communications systems for which friendly force military capabilities were not designed. Such challenges mean that intelligence analysis during urban contingencies relies more on human intelligence (HUMINT) than is the norm. As CSS units are among the most dispersed and omnipresent in any area of operations, their soldiers are potentially valuable intelligence collectors. Men and women assigned to guard depots or other facilities will quickly become very familiar with the area around their posts and the routines associated with that terrain. Intelligence analysts too seldom take advantage of these assets; rarely are such individuals informed of their intelligence roles, trained to perform them effectively, and incorporated into a comprehensive HUMINT-collection system. The potential benefits are considerable for organizations that capitalize on this potential, but there will also be a corresponding increase in the administrative and reporting burden born by CSS organizations as they consolidate and pass the valuable information on to potential users.

Guards are not the only soldiers who should be better incorporated into U.S. urban collection efforts. CSS drivers, men and women manning water purification sites, and others with frequent noncombatant contact should all receive training as intelligence collectors. They need to know their intelligence reporting responsibilities (e.g., reporting the locations of potentially useful resources in the urban area and understanding and remembering the commander's critical information requirements (CCIR), priority intelligence requirements (PIR), and other mission needs). They should know what to report, how to report, and how to determine whether information merits being passed on immediately or instead transmitted after mission completion. They should have the equipment necessary to render reports. Such preparations will consume both training and operational time. As in the case of guard personnel, CSS headquarters will have to process incoming reports, determine which are of internal use, which should be forwarded, and which can be cast aside. Reports will have to be monitored, compiled, consolidated, and disseminated to not only intelligence nodes but also operational units with an immediate need to see specific items. The inordinate reliance on HUMINT magnifies the role of the CSS soldier as intelligence collector during urban operations. Neither the benefits nor the costs have heretofore been fully recognized.

CSS units share many of the many above challenges with other types of military organizations. The ways in which urban areas impact CSS operations differ in character and degree; in some cases combat, combat support, and combat service support units will be able to benefit from a given adaptation, in others they will not. The following section addresses approaches to meeting the challenges via (1) promoting anticipation and adaptation, (2) integrating CSS C4ISR operations with others in the force, and (3) preparing for extraordinary CSS urban operations difficulties.

PRIMARY APPROACHES TO MEETING THESE URBAN CSS CHALLENGES

> The nature of urban operations creates unique support demands. The quantities of supplies required will differ from other types of operations, as will the types and amount of medical services required. Forces will need reconstitution more frequently. All movement will entail more risk and be more difficult to accomplish. Sustaining bases may not be possible, or may be difficult to secure. Support requirements to [host nation] and civilian agencies will likely be much greater than in other operations, and may be the focus of the urban operation itself. Support activities will play a large role in the transition phase of joint urban operations (JUOs).
>
> Joint Publication (JP) 3-06, *Joint Urban Operations*

The many CSS challenges associated with urban operations require innovation, initiative, flexibility, and maintenance of a "big picture" perspective by leaders at all echelons. Situations will change quickly. The consequences of seemingly small actions will have repercussions that could affect strategic decisions and the success of an entire operation. Succeeding as a combat service support leader will require an understanding of:

- How his or her force can appropriately anticipate and adapt to the constant change that characterizes urban actions.

- The nature of command and control in the urban environment.

- The otherwise extraordinary demands that are commonplace when a unit operates in a village, town, or city.

Promoting Anticipation and Adaptation

Anticipation and rapid adaptation are interrelated keys to success during urban undertakings. Both require savvy synchronization of centralized and decentralized control. They also demand constant review of current doctrine and a willingness to step outside its guidance when the situation so demands.

The wide dispersion of CSS personnel that characterizes virtually any urban operation means that drivers, medical providers, or vehicle recovery specialists will frequently have a better feel for conditions on the streets than will those who spend most of their time in a command post. It is they who will therefore have the current information needed to anticipate and adapt most effectively, just as theirs will be the requirement to do so most quickly. On the other hand, the low density of some CSS assets (e.g., one medic per infantry platoon) means that control of such resources at times has to be more centralized than is otherwise the norm, in order to meet short-notice mission requirements. The following several paragraphs consider ways to address this potential tension between decentralization and centralization to best meet the need to anticipate and adapt.

Decentralization. As has been mentioned, the ubiquity of noncombatant eyes in any town or city poses a security risk for CSS personnel. Remaining in one location too long allows the enemy to determine patterns of behavior and assess friendly force vulnerabilities. For large support enterprises, sizable base camps manned with constant and vigilant security might be the appropriate response. For more limited activities, however, frequent movement may be the more feasible security measure. Smaller units cannot secure an area sufficiently large to deny an adversary observation or engagement by direct fire systems. Such outposts lack the manpower to maintain both the requisite 24-hour security and the standard of support expected of them.

No friendly force activity should be considered safe from attack during urban operations. Panamanian paramilitary forces and deserters attacked marked ambulances during Operation Just Cause. Such routine and seemingly mundane activities as resupply of Class I (subsistence items such as food) or garbage disposal can be targeted as part of a preplanned strike, by an opportunistic enemy spotting a lost convoy, or by noncombatants driven by deprivation. Traffic stoppages, either deliberate for the purpose of ambush or due to more innocent reasons, make U.S. vehicles vulnerable targets. Junior leaders, even individual vehicle drivers, will have to understand the necessity of constantly monitoring the tactical situation, assessing risk, and deviating from plans when the situation demands. With such decentralization in decisionmaking comes the implication that tables of organization and equipment (TOE) or habitual task organizations might need modification. There may be a need to equip every convoy with a radio, cell phone, or other means of making its location and status known.[8] A system as simple as equipping vehicles with a location transmitter and a means for the driver to send a status code (e.g., green = situation nonthreatening, amber = require assistance, time not imminent, red = immediate assistance essential) might be sufficient in lieu of providing voice communications. Yet it must be remembered that, barring overhead or other retransmission capabilities, any such system will suffer the same interruptions as do radio and GPS communications due to breaks in LOS and electrical interference.

Decentralization during urban operations need not be limited to U.S. Army-internal activities. Coalition, interagency, and interservice undertakings can likewise benefit from tolerance of less top-down control. Traditional conceptualizations of coalition partnerships often envision each participant as a self-contained, standalone entity capable of providing all services needed to sustain its own force. This approach can lead to unnecessary redundancy when viewing an operation from a coalition-wide perspective. Efficiency might be increased were nations to enter into agreements in which various coalition members provide forces on a functional basis. Alternatively, coalition members can pool resources such as transportation assets and maintenance personnel, thereby reducing deployment requirements. The closer proximity in which units find themselves

---

[8]Since operations in Somalia during the early 1990s, most units have required that a convoy include at least one vehicle with a radio. Kevin Born email to Russell W. Glenn, "Updated CSS UO Study Comments," October 15, 2002.

during urban operations can make such options more feasible than in other environments.

Military, PVO, NGO, and even commercial enterprises can also mutually benefit from a sharing of responsibilities. PVO and NGO in particular often enter a theater with many of the same objectives sought by U.S. military forces in their interactions with noncombatants: relief of hunger, provision of health care, and assistance in developing local resources. The British Army has made progress in cooperative ventures with some such organizations. Predeployment training at Catterick Garrison in Yorkshire at times includes PVO representatives. The U.S. armed services would be well advised to consider similar team building and expand on it to the benefit of the armed services, nonmilitary organizations, and civilians in operational areas by sharing the burden of care. Such organizations will be in a theater regardless of the military's preferences. And because supporting entire urban populations is well beyond the capability of most deployed forces, such an initiative might be viewed as making the best out of a situation over which military leaders in any case have little control. The approach will involve new mindsets and some assumption of risk. Security will inevitably be a concern. Even the best-intentioned PVO or NGO might inadvertently compromise security (e.g., by revealing that a U.S. commander has barred use of a particular route the next day, thereby unwittingly revealing the objective of a pending offensive action). Such risks can be minimized with practice and a building of trust. Alternatively, some PVOs and NGOs believe (with justification in many contingencies) that too close a relationship with the military can compromise their appearance of neutrality in dealings with the public and opposing factions. There are benefits and risks for both sides when attempting to establish relationships between military and aid organizations. It must be determined whether the potential benefits override negative repercussions.

Divisions of responsibility along functional lines have in the past precipitated contractual relationships between coalition members. Operations in East Timor and its capital city of Dili are a case in point. The Australians found that contracts between coalition militaries abetted overall cooperation in many instances. Unfortunately the "payment for services" occasionally took on an absurd character and became a divisive element. Writing after the successful operations in Dili and other parts of East Timor, an Australian officer noted that

> The issue [of contractual relationships] was a serious one—squabbles over basic supplies have the potential to fracture a coalition. Australian operational culture, based on considerable war fighting experience, reflects the immediate needs of the force: provide the support as required and then worry about the details. The experience of working with the [Association of Southeast Asian Nations] countries demonstrated that this was not how they "did business." Rather, "they wanted to do deals like a normal commercial arrangement before you gave them the logistic support and in some sense they seem to even forget that we're doing that in an operational environment." The South Koreans even sought compensation when a ration delivery was late on the basis that Australia had not upheld its end of the contractual relationship. They also billed Australia for the water consumed by our liaison officer . . . Australian fuel pumps did not have meters on them; it was therefore not easy to measure accurately how much fuel was provided to other contingents . . . In fact, despite requiring the contingents to arrive in Australia self-sufficient for a minimum of 42 days, a large number of contingents, bordering on the majority, have arrived with very little by way of their own logistic support with them, and no ability to do any kind of independent sustainment of themselves . . . They pretty much have brought nothing.[9]

Fortunately, formalities such as contracts are often replaced with mutual trust and a handshake at lower echelons.[10]

Urban operations will demand much of the CSS soldier at every echelon. As with his or her combat and combat support counterparts, training that emphasizes initiative exercised within the constraints of the commander's intent is an essential prerequisite to commitment to operations in a city. Yet while many CSS aspects of urban undertakings will demand decentralized individual and small-unit actions, the scarcity of support elements will force leaders to carefully monitor and at times centralize a force's providers.

---

[9]Alan Ryan, *Primary Responsibilities and Primary Risks: Australian Defence Force Participation in the International Force East Timor,* Australian Land Warfare Studies Centre Study Paper No. 304, November 2000, pp. 106–107.

[10]Born email, "Updated CSS UO Study Comments."

Centralization. While much in the urban environment favors a more decentralized approach to operations, there are also many aspects of operations in which centralization is advisable if limited resources are to be used most effectively. The compartmented nature of urban operations at the lowest echelons means that very junior leaders will have to make decisions on their own. However, this tendency to decentralize decisionmaking at the tactical level is matched by pressures to centralize scarce resources.

Movement during an attack is generally parallel to the axis of advance, but minimizing exposure to enemy fire means that such movement is through buildings or underground rather than in the streets. Travel in the open is limited to dashes across streets from building to building. Friendly units to the right and left may be sighted only in glimpses because of walls, buildings, or other obstacles to line-of-sight. Higher-echelon leaders therefore have to trust the judgment of subordinates in charge of the small elements moving forward against the foe. But the same obstacles that block lateral vision will at times also prevent rapid movement between axes and block reliable communications between elements operating in parallel. Lateral reinforcement or resupply is therefore problematic.

An asset (e.g., a medic) accompanying one unit in the advance will find that movement to assist another could involve a long retracing of steps and then an advance along the second axis of roughly equal length. The radio call requesting the support of that asset might never get through. TOE allocations of but one medic per infantry platoon might therefore prove inadequate when several walls, floors, or fire-swept city streets separate squads. CSS commanders will have to consider weighting main efforts to an extent greater than is the norm.

Consolidating medics from uncommitted platoons and sending them forward with unfamiliar squads is one solution. Keeping medics (or other similarly scarce resources) back and sending them forward only when needed is another. The first course of action improves medical responsiveness but may mean that medics are passed from unit to unit as exhaustion demands forward passages of line to keep fresh soldiers at the cutting edge (fresh other than the increasingly exhausted medics). The second preserves a well-rested pool of aid-givers. Yet even the short distances between where the pool is kept and the locations of wounded can cause vital moments to be lost. This is especially true given the difficulty of navigating through tortuous inner building routes, perhaps with very limited visibility. And, again, calls for assistance might not reach back through buildings and walls between forward elements and the medics' location.

Similarly difficult decisions will confront commanders faced with high consumption rates for water, ammunition, Class VIII (medical materials), and other items, though in these cases forecasting needed replenishment is sometimes possible (unlike predicting when a man will be wounded or injured). Regardless, there are strong arguments in support of breaking habitual relationships so as to enhance cross-boundary surge capacity. Support operations involving aid to non-combatants might similarly demand consolidating limited assets in nontraditional ways. Leaders will have to remember that CSS personnel will require frequent rest and rotation just as do those in maneuver units. This will be especially troublesome when dealing with assets likely already in short supply.

It has been noted that combat units in built-up areas will frequently task organize in smaller elements than they do in other environments. Infantry units maneuvering as squads and vehicles task-organized individually or in pairs are not unusual. Supporting the resultant greater number of nodes will tend to promote organizing CSS units in smaller components similarly and giving their leaders greater say in their operations, allowing them to properly respond to immediate tactical demands. Yet the greater number of nodes means that providers will have to be more efficient if they are to adequately support all in need, a tendency that will encourage retaining close control and higher-level oversight of limited CSS resources.

The presence of large numbers of noncombatants and the closeness of friendly forces to one another will necessitate centralized control of other operations as well, activities of which CSS units will be a vital part. Psychological operations (PSYOP) and deception efforts must be synchronized if they are to be successful; the actions of every unit have to support PSYOP objectives or a deception story. Constant surveillance by members of the urban population means that inconsistencies are more likely to compromise these efforts than in more sparsely populated areas. Intelligence collection and analysis similarly need to be centrally managed in a manner that best serves the needs of the entire force as well as its individual components. (It should be noted that the assignment of PSYOP and civil affairs personnel to CSS units of battalion and greater size could pay significant dividends. In addition to their ability to influence indigenous civilians' willingness to provide intelligence, operations in Haiti demonstrated that these individuals can reduce loss of friendly force materials to theft and sabotage.)[11]

Finding the appropriate balance between centralization and decentralization of CSS assets will be a major undertaking for support leaders. There will too often be no good solution, only better or worse ones. All will involve varying amounts and types of risk. METT-TC (Mission, Enemy, Terrain and weather, Troops and support available, Time available, and Civilian considerations) analysis will be essential. The unique demands of an urban area will at times considerably complicate that analysis.

Further thoughts on promoting anticipation and adaptation. There are myriad other ways in which CSS personnel will have to anticipate and adapt to rapidly changing urban conditions. Some can be foreseen even before deployment: requisitioning extra tires to account for excessive urban wear and tear, determining how to react to the sudden formation of a crowd desperate for the food being distributed, or specifying what to do to avoid violating taboos should female members of a particularly sensitive group appear for medical care when only male medics are present. For other contingencies such prescience will be impossible; the best the provider can do is to maintain maximum flexibility during planning and execution. Doctrine may provide guidance; often it will not. FM 3-06.11[12] provides the following as basic initial advice:

- Preconfigure resupply loads and push them forward at every opportunity (though it should be noted that the lean force structures of many CSS units mean that the personnel and material-

---

[11]Ibid.

[12]*Combat Service Support,* Field Manual 3-06.11, Chapter 13, *http://155.217.58/cgi-bin/atdl.dll/fm/3-06.11/ch13.htm,* pp. 13-1 to 13-2.

handling equipment necessary for such processes might be unavailable in a theater or area of operations).[13]

- Provide supplies to using units in required quantities as close as
  possible to the location where those supplies are needed.

- Protect supplies and CSS elements from the effects of enemy fire
  both by making use of cover and avoiding detection.

- Disperse and decentralize CSS elements with proper emphasis
  on communication, command and control, security, and
  proximity of main supply route (MSR) for resupply.

- Plan for carrying parties and litter bearers.

- Plan for and use host country support and civil resources when
  practical.

- Position support units as far forward as the tactical situation
  permits.

- Plan for requesting and distributing special equipment such as
  toggle ropes with grappling hooks, ladders, and hand tools.
  Wearing body armor will likely be the norm.

- Position support units near drop or landing zones (DZ/LZ) so
  that resupply involves the minimum necessary interim surface
  movement.

There is legitimate concern that the current distribution-based U.S.
Army supply system might be inadequate to the demands of urban
contingencies. Such a system relies heavily on reasonably accurate
prediction of requirements and sufficient responsiveness to demands. The many factors that can suddenly and significantly alter a
situation during any type of urban operation mean that such prediction is problematic. That urban areas are difficult places to secure
supply caches or deliver loads quickly further complicates the issue,
as does the virtually complete absence of historical data on urban
consumption rates. It will behoove CSS commanders to have those
items most likely to be needed on short notice prepared to move
forward before they are called for (e.g., certain ammunition types,
water, and medical supplies). It similarly would benefit all parts of

---

[13]Ibid.

the service were CSS staffs to maintain usage records so that the current deficiency in historical data is rectified as quickly as possible.

As is the case in any military undertaking, it is important to constantly bear in mind that adaptation is never ending. Adversaries adapt constantly, as do noncombatant groups and other parties that influence operations. The close proximity of these many players in urban environments means that they will more frequently observe each other and that communications between parties will be quicker than when distances are greater and the density of ways of communicating is less. Advantage will lie with the force that anticipates better, that adapts more quickly, and that seeks to disrupt a foe's ability to respond effectively to changes. Adaptation is not merely a case of observation and adjustment. It entails surveillance, consolidating those observations, making major or fine adjustments as necessary, and seeking to cause the enemy to adapt improperly, too slowly, or not at all.

Organizations that learn well will be more successful. As such, U.S. forces that maintain a means of rapidly accumulating and disseminating lessons learned should be better at adaptation than those that do not.[14]

The Nature of Command and Control: Integration of CSS and C4ISR Operations

> In my day, as a junior leader, my decisions had an immediate impact on my troops and the enemy. In today's military operations the decisions of junior leaders still have those immediate impacts, but modern telecommunications can also magnify every incident, put every incident under a media microscope, and send

---

[14]The literature on "learning organizations" and the need for disseminating lessons learned in the Army is fairly extensive. Perhaps the best-known book on the first is Peter M. Senge, *The Fifth Discipline: The Art & Practice of the Learning Organization,* New York: Doubleday, 1994. At the macro level, the U.S. Army's Center for Army Lessons Learned is a notable resource for sharing information. Much of its work is available on the World Wide Web at *http://call.army.mil.* However, units at all echelons need to have a formal means of internally collecting pertinent lessons and providing them to those who can make use of them in a timely fashion. Training, the use of debriefings, and a means of getting the word out are all part of the process involved in establishing and maintaining such a capability.

descriptions and images of every incident instantly around the world for scores of experts and commentators to interpret for millions of viewers and listeners. Thus the decisions of junior leaders and the actions of their small teams can influence the course of international affairs.

General Peter Cosgrove, Australian Army

The pace of urban operations is such that anything but complete, real-time integration of CSS planning with that of other service and joint components will threaten mission failure. Logistics and other support elements will find that they might simultaneously be involved in the support, stability, and combat operations that together comprise USMC General Charles C. Krulak's "three block war."[15] There are in fact scenarios in which logistics concerns will dominate operational objectives. These contingencies might merit CSS officers assuming the lead role while combat and combat support organizations serve in a supporting rather than supported status. Leaders, training, and doctrine should all account for such possibilities now so that the Army is prepared for them. Just as the U.S. Army's Task Force Hawk found itself in a supporting role during the air campaign in the Balkans, so might tradition be turned on its head during all or phases of future support and stability operations. The infantryman might deploy to support the medic providing care, engineer building a school, or quartermaster distributing food and water.

Regardless of whether an operation falls under CSS leadership or not, urban undertakings will demand greater, more assertive, and better-integrated CSS expertise at the start of and throughout the command

---

[15]General Krulak described the future challenges confronting Americans on the battlefield as follows: "This is the landscape upon which the 21st Century battle will be fought. It will be an asymmetrical battlefield. Much like the Germanic tribes, our enemies will not allow us to fight the Son of Desert Storm, but will try to draw us into the stepchild of Chechnya. In one moment in time, our service members will be feeding and clothing displaced refugees—providing humanitarian assistance. In the next moment, they will be holding two warring tribes apart—conducting peacekeeping operations—and, finally, they will be fighting a highly lethal mid-intensity battle—all on the same day . . . all within three city blocks. It will be what we call the 'three block war.'" From "Draft Remarks for The National Press Club 10 October 1997 by Gen. Charles C. Krulak," downloadable at *http://www.usmc.mil/cmcspeeches.nsf/f9c9e7a1fe 55fe42852564280078b406/6f38a0fe88a127fa85256530006f3951*, accessed February 5, 2003.

estimate and Intelligence Preparation of the Battlefield (IPB) processes. At present, CSS planning is too often executed parallel to but
separately from the planning for maneuver activities. Too frequently
the combat arms guidance to CSS elements consists of little more
than describing the maneuver plan and instructing the providers to
maintain adequate support. The potentially shorter tactical reaction
times and a physical environment that tends to impede CSS responsiveness makes such *laissez faire* attitudes a danger to mission success. Better understanding of each other's respective communities is
called for. Communications, training, and equipment need to be
compatible. Decisions that impact local conditions and the political
situation will require evaluation from a common perspective. For
example, an embargo on petroleum products was lifted after U.S.
Army forces entered Haiti in the 1990s and a less repressive regime
assumed the reins of government. Few civilian vehicles had moved
on the streets of Port-au-Prince when fuel was scarce, so that, as an
American officer recalled, "movements of U.S. forces throughout the
city were unimpeded. This changed almost overnight once fuel
supplies became available, making it very difficult for a [Quick Reaction Force] to reach the scene of an incident unless they were transported by helicopter."[16]

Combat service support elements need to have the same maps,
overhead imagery, and communications capabilities of the other
arms. In the absence of maps with appropriate scales, overhead
photos or other imagery will be called for. Gridlines and graphical
information added to the raw products must be consistent across all
branches and units. Similarly, logistics and other supporting units
(e.g., engineers) tend to have less in the way of communications
capabilities than do many maneuver units, especially with regard to
equipment capable of secure communications. Observers at U.S.
training centers repeatedly comment that a friendly force plan can
be as readily compromised by discussions at the squad level of a CSS
or combat support (CS) unit as any other, yet the problem persists.

Just as CSS operations are a component of the greater Combat–
Combat Support–Combat Service Support system, the many ele-

---

[16]Kevin Born observations on reading Lawrence E. Casper's *Falcon Brigade: Combat
and Command in Somalia and Haiti,* Boulder, CO: Lynne Rienner, 2001.

ments that together comprise CSS are also part of the combat service support system. Each of these CSS system parts are themselves systems in their own right, consisting of interrelated functions, capabilities, services, and items that interact to provide end products of one form or another. CSS and its components are therefore systems within systems. Just as a force will operate suboptimally if CSS is not fully integrated with combat and combat support functions, so will CSS fail to reach its full potential if transport, supply, legal, chaplain, and its many other parts do not orchestrate their plans and actions.

Keeping this system-of-systems relationship in mind will be especially useful during urban operations. Villages, towns, and cities are also interdependent and interactive systems within systems. When a military force enters an urban area, its leaders would do well to contemplate how their units (systems) will influence and be affected by those of the urban environment. Envisioning desired end states in the sense of systems will assist planners in understanding how military operations can favorably or negatively influence attainment of their ultimate objectives. To use an example to which this study will refer on several occasions, a desired end state might include a stable urban economy consistent with pre-conflict income levels. Given this objective, planners should consider how they might work to preclude the inflation that their forces, PVOs, NGOs, and other outsiders will introduce by independently competing for indigenous resources rather than cooperatively agreeing to a pricing scheme. Nor are the potential negative consequences limited to economic ones. During operations in Rwanda, an NGO hired medically qualified personnel who had been working in a local government clinic, thereby depriving that indigenous capability of the expertise it needed to support the local population.[17] Similarly, outside aid providers need to ensure that their activities do not consume an undue share of local resources such as water, suitable land, or transportation.[18]

---

[17]Elspeth C. Ritchie and Robert Mott, "Caring for Civilians During Peace Keeping Missions: Priorities and Decisions," *Military Medicine* 167 (Supplement 3, 2002), p. 145.

[18]Ibid.

Such significant economic concerns might qualify as key or even vital "terrain." A coordinating draft of FM 3-20.96, *RSTA Squadron*, cites the following as possibly rating such designation:[19]

- Safe havens

- Hospitals

- Police stations

- Embassies

- Hazardous areas

- Construction sites

- Dangerous intersections

- Bridges

- Criminal areas

- Major terrain features

- Parks

- Industrial complexes

- Airports

Despite the examples given, the wise CSS planner will not restrain his analysis by limiting the concept of "key terrain" to physical features alone. It could include religious leaders, heads of family, or individuals who control vital resources, influence others, or facilitate activities critical to people's livelihoods. Other features—economic, social, and cultural—will likewise sometimes attain such status. (In other RAND urban work, these many points of mission importance are designated as "critical points." They include centers of gravity, decisive points, and others defined as "geographic points or other elements that could have an extraordinary influence on the achievement of objectives."[20])

---

[19]Field Manual 3-20.96, *RSTA Squadron* (2nd Coordinating Draft), U.S. Army Armor Center, June 12, 2001, pp. 7-13 to 7-14.

[20]For further discussion of critical points, see Russell W. Glenn, "Urban Combat Is Complex," *Naval Institute Proceedings* 128 (February 2002), pp. 62–65; or Russell W.

Preparing for Extraordinary CSS Urban Operations Difficulties

> The density of noncombatants is the single greatest influence on logistic support. In combat, this concentration of civilians can add a considerable support requirement. In [military operations other than war], provision of support to noncombatants may be the primary focus of the operation. *All six joint logistic functional areas— supply, maintenance, transportation, civil engineering, health services, and other services—are likely to be taxed to support noncombatants in [Joint Urban Operations].* Other services will probably include above-average requirements for such capabilities as waste disposal, contracting, mortuary services, and civil administration, to name but a few.
>
> JP 3-06, *Joint Urban Operations,* September 2002
> (emphasis in original)

The greater density of demands, separation of units requiring support, and physical challenges related to urban operations will increase the time between requests for service and supporting units' abilities to respond. These physical challenges include the difficulty of urban navigation, compartmented nature of the terrain, and higher consumption rates. Issues associated with civilians in the area of operations can considerably add to and complicate the burden on CSS units. Moral obligations have always dictated that America's warriors attempt to minimize the suffering by persons unfortunate enough to find themselves trapped by war. The influence of the media and related domestic and international intolerance for suffering lend added incentive, were any needed. Perhaps too often overlooked, there are also operational reasons to seek civilian goodwill. Support from elements of the population or their withholding of support for an adversary can be decisive. Stated differently, the noncombatant population is a potential resource, one that could serve as a source of intelligence, provide contacts with key indigenous personnel, supply willing labor, and hopefully sustain a supportive postoperation government.

Glenn, *Visualizing the Elephant: Managing Complexity During Military Urban Operations,* Santa Monica, CA; RAND, DB-430-A, forthcoming.

Indigenous noncombatants. A number of factors complicate CSS interactions with urban noncombatants. The native civilian population is not homogenous in character or attitude toward the friendly force (or, for that matter, the enemy). Earlier RAND work proposes that a Continuum of Relative Interest be employed as an analytic tool to monitor civilian dispositions. Unlike previous oversimplifications that consider operational actors as either friendly, neutral, or enemy, the new tool employs the broader spectrum of "Ally-Accomplice-Neutral-Obstacle-Adversary."[21] It is recognized that attitudes are not constant over time and that a particular group can have components that do not share those of the group as a whole. The continuum helps the CSS planner by providing a measure of how willing given actors might be to assist the friendly force. Further, the continuum assists the user in gauging force protection needs, identifying antipathies between population sectors, and measuring required levels of support (e.g., during a mission involving the supply of food, water, or other essentials).[22]

Support for noncombatants will not end with the cessation of hostilities. Arguably the most intensive urban combat during America's involvement in the Vietnam War was that during and following the 1968 Tet offensive. The official Marine Corps history described the formidable task facing U.S. and Army of the Republic of Vietnam (ARVN) forces in Hue as the city was retaken:

> One other problem that the allies faced was population control. With the widespread destruction in the city, the estimated 116,000 homeless had to be fed and temporarily housed. . . . [There were] 5,000 refugees in a Catholic church and another 17,000 at Hue University. Another 40,000 displaced people were in the Citadel sector. [The local subsector advisor, U.S. Army Major Jack E.] Walker initially concerned himself with three tasks: restoring city services including water and power; eliminating health hazards including burying the dead; and securing food. With the assistance of the local Catholic hierarchy and American resources and personnel, Walker and his people began attacking all of these problems . . . . In

---

[21]Jamison Jo Medby and Russell W. Glenn, *Street Smart: IPB for Urban Operations,* Santa Monica, CA: RAND, 2002.

[22]For further discussion of the Continuum of Relative Interests, see Medby, *Street Smart.*

the first two weeks there was hardly any semblance of public order . . . . Thievery and looting were widespread. War victims stole from their fellow sufferers. All deserted houses were emptied of valuables. Robbed victims sought to steal from others.[23]

The recently superseded U.S. Army's Field Manual (FM) 90-10-1, *An Infantryman's Guide to Combat in Built-Up Areas*, specifically warned that

> Commanders at all levels automatically assume the burden of ensuring the bare necessities of life to all civilian noncombatants that fall under their control during [military operations on urbanized terrain]. Depending on the situation, protection, food, water, shelter and medical care may be provided in special refuges established for that purpose, or they may be provided in place by some other organization. Whatever the final arrangement, U.S. commanders should expect to exercise control and provide support until long-term arrangements can be made.[24]

The advice remains relevant.

Private volunteer and nongovernmental organizations (PVOs/ NGOs). The alliance of U.S. military forces and Catholic agencies in relieving the suffering of Hue's residents' offers a lesson too rarely considered. CSS forces are very seldom given sufficient resources to adequately support both their comrades in arms and local civilians. Joining forces with NGO and PVO can be an effective means of addressing this shortfall, but the opportunity is seldom handled effectively. As noted earlier, the civil-military operations center is the doctrinal mechanism for coordinating the many nongovernmental and private groups in an area of operations. Its de facto effects too often consist of little more than monitoring various agencies' status, frequently because of a lack of cooperation among them. Even such limited interactions have been sources of friction. U.S. or coalition success can be influenced by PVO/NGO operations for both better

[23]Jack Shulimson, Leonard A. Blasiol, Charles R. Smith, and David A. Dawson, *U.S. Marines in Vietnam, the Defining Year, 1968,* Washington, D.C.: History and Museums Division, Headquarters, U.S. Marine Corps, 1997, pp. 219–221.

[24]United States Army, FM 90-10-1, *An Infantryman's Guide to Combat in Built-Up Areas, with Change 1,* October 3, 1995, p. G-5. Accessed at *http://www.globalsecurity. org/military/library/policy/army/fm/90-10-1/appg.pdf* on October 1, 2002.

and worse. During multinational peace operations in East Timor, at least 65 PVO or NGO were involved, 23 of which were United Nations agencies. Yet the UN Office for Coordination of Humanitarian Assistance in Timor lacked the requisite logistical expertise to coordinate and control even its own agencies. Further, the nature of the United Nations is such that separate UN organizations can participate in operations with little coordination between them or their management. As a result of these two conditions, the various aid providers struck out on their own to pursue actions not coordinated by any central oversight, UN or otherwise.[25] The quality of this care and the behavior of NGO and PVO members left much to be desired. NGOs "were justly criticized for being slow to react, uncoordinated, lacking forward planning and misapplying assets. One FALANTIL [Timor's pro-independence militia] commander stated that many members of NGO made a bad impression on the local population by their waste, inefficiency, and inappropriate displays of wealth. The local population often perceived them to be pursuing their own agendas with little consideration of the actual needs of the community."[26] That such adverse perceptions by the indigenous population can undermine friendly force initiatives is obvious, especially if all outsiders are viewed as a common "they." The issue is complicated in that such organizations are frequently in theater prior to the arrival of a coalition and thus lack even an informal coordination mechanism.

The threats to friendly force personnel and operational freedom of action can also be more immediate and direct. During operations in Somalia during January 1993, an NGO chose to establish a grain distribution point in close proximity to a U.S. logistics base, giving rise to concerns about increased traffic and the security of the installation as civilians gathered just outside the base gate while waiting for grain.[27]

Security concerns, differences in ways of operating, and fears that collaboration will be misperceived by locals or outside observers mean that the seams along which military and these other agencies make contact are generally sources of friction rather than links in a

---

[25]Ryan, *Primary Responsibilities*, pp. 108, 110.

[26]Ibid., p. 109.

[27]Ibid.

cooperative effort. While military leaders will seldom be able to directly control the behavior of these other support elements in a theater, they should have procedures in place to promote cooperation, encourage support of common goals, and minimize interference with operational objectives.

Contractors. A third group of noncombatants with whom CSS personnel will have extensive contact are contractors, both indigenous and others. Civilian commercial organizations have long been an integral part of U.S. force buildups. Contract personnel are now taking on an increasing role involving systems directly supporting and sustaining combat operations. Contractors can be fundamental to an operation's success or failure given the absolute reliance on such personnel's expertise for some skills and equipment support. They will influence an operation from reception through the post-redeployment rebuilding of civilian infrastructure. Like PVOs and NGOs, their efforts should be synchronized with military objectives. The security risks involved in the employment of contract personnel are similar to those arising with the aid organizations. This creates a tension that has to be resolved so that the needs of both mission accomplishment and operations security requirements are met. In addition, the likelihood that some CSS support activities will be within a few blocks of the line of contact means that these civilians might well be at considerable risk during urban contingencies. While many contractors have demonstrated personal bravery under similar circumstances in the past, it is essential that mission accomplishment not rely on the assumption that such behavior will inevitably be demonstrated. A possible solution is to require contractors to serve as reservists who can then be brought on active duty for the duration of an operation.[28]

POSTOPERATION RECOVERY

CSS planners and commanders will be integral to the transition from ongoing operations to redeployment and post-hostility activities. At some point, generally well before the cessation of hostilities, the character of incoming personnel and materiel should shift to that

---

[28]Born email, "Updated CSS UO Study Comments." See also Edward G. Keating, *Compensating Civilians on the Battlefield,* Santa Monica, CA: RAND, 1993.

needed to prepare the military force for return to home base and assist the host nation in transitioning to peace. The latter will often incorporate much in the way of rebuilding both physical and human infrastructure. The ease of that transition and the strength of the peace will both be influenced by how well the friendly force demonstrates concern for the welfare of the indigenous population. Cities in particular might have large concentrations of civilians lacking shelter, sufficient sustenance, and medical care. Provision of these resources will initially take a backseat to combat operations. Afterward, however, the local and international perception will be that the friendly force should immediately redress suffering in the areas under their control. Properly selecting the point in time at which to begin transitioning from shipments of combat-specific materiel and personnel to those that will be in demand after the fighting has stopped will greatly affect urban population suffering and (potentially) worldwide perceptions of an operation's success.

CONCLUSION

Regardless of the CSS functional area, the ability to anticipate and adapt, to function as a full-fledged member of the command structure, and to be ready to handle the extraordinary demands that characterize urban operations will all be essential preconditions to success. Soldiers in each functional area will also face tasks that have specific impacts on their ability to accomplish their missions. It is to these that we turn in the remainder of the report.

THE NEXT STEP: FUNCTIONAL AREA ANALYSIS

The challenges associated with urban operations will influence the lives of every CSS soldier. The approaches to dealing with these challenges—anticipation and effective adaptation, well-conceived C^3, and handling the sometimes extraordinary character of missions conducted in villages, towns, and cities—will succeed or fail depending on how well those individual soldiers are prepared. "Big picture" considerations have dominated discussion to this point. In the chapters that follow, we look at more specific adjustments, factors necessary to address issues regarding the functional areas of concern to the CSS community. As with the general approaches we have just discussed, there are a number of desired goals that will be a part of any solution. Several, the products of ongoing initiatives and past research, are listed below and incorporated in the analysis:

- Reduced weight and size for deployment and reduced signature purposes

- Shorter deployment times

- More efficient operations (i.e., get more from the same quantity of resources previously needed to accomplish a function)

- More effective operations (i.e., achieving better results with the same quantity of resources)

- Meet the full range of operational demands

- Reduce the number of friendly force and noncombatant personnel killed, wounded, or suffering psychological injuries

- Facilitate restoring the environment to the pre-operation or an even more desirable state

- Include consideration of the second- and higher-order effects of decisions or actions.

On occasion, the investigation of functional areas will encompass long-range initiatives or technological developments. On the whole, however, the focus is more limited with respect to time, concentrating on the present and roughly the next decade. Those systems already fielded or likely to enter the U.S. Army inventory during the period of SBCT fielding and early employment receive the bulk of attention.[29]

The functional areas selected for analysis are:

- Arming

---

[29]From *http://www.army.mil/features/strykeroe/*: "The Stryker Brigade Combat Team (SBCT) is designed to bridge the gap between The Army's light and heavy forces. The unit provides combatant commanders increased operational and tactical flexibility. The Stryker, an eight-wheeled medium weight armored vehicle, is the SBCT's primary combat and combat support platform. Significantly lighter and more transportable than existing tanks and armored vehicles, the Stryker fulfills an immediate requirement to equip a strategically and tactically deployable brigade, capable of rapid movement worldwide."

- Manning

- Sustaining and moving

- Fixing

- Other (liaison, EOD, vehicle design, and general engineering)

- Security, force protection, and safety

Where it is logical to do so, each discussion will follow the sequence used above to introduce the three approaches: anticipation and adaptation, C^3, and extraordinary demands related to undertakings in built-up areas.

Chapter Three

ARMING

If my men put any more ammunition into the city, we would have sunk it.

Major General William F. Garrison,
Task Force Ranger Commander, Mogadishu, Somalia,
referring to actions of October 3–4, 1993

Urban combat has historically proved to be a voracious consumer of Class V supplies (ammunition), in particular small arms ammunition and hand grenades. There is no reason to believe that selected Class V consumption rates will not continue to be high in future urban contingencies. During periods of sustained intense urban combat, smoke (to provide concealment when crossing enemy engagement areas), demolitions (for breaching obstacles, gaining entry into structures, or toppling buildings), small arms ammunition, grenades, and booby-traps are likely to be among the items needed in quantities that exceed those for other terrain. Those making pre-operation estimates should not unthinkingly rely on what little historical consumption data are available, however. Rules of engagement (ROE) driven by a high level of concern for noncombatant casualties or infrastructure damage could alter the types of Class V that are most readily consumed (e.g., flash-bang rather than fragmentation grenades may be called for more often). It is unlikely that World War II urban combat tactics precipitating destruction of large swaths of urban terrain and mass civilian casualties will be the norm during future conflicts. Nonetheless, CSS planners should remember that strict ROE designed to preserve noncombatant life and civilian infrastructure have more than once gone by the wayside when enemy resistance rendered such a desirable approach too costly in friendly force lives. Fighting in 1945 Manila, in which early limitations on the use of indirect fire were relaxed when U.S. casualties began to mount, is one such instance. FM 90-10-1 (since redesignated FM 3-06.11) provides some assistance to those tasked with making initial consumption estimates for urban operations. It outlines the types of materials, including munitions, that the U.S. Army Infantry School expects to have a high usage rate during urban action. The manual recommends that logisticians plan for ammunition usage at four times normal consumption rates.[1]

Not only will planners have to ensure that greater quantities of selected ammunition are stored in a theater, they will also have to determine how this increased tonnage is to be moved forward and secured during urban contingencies. The desirability of attacking ammunition convoys has already been mentioned. Ammunition points could prove lucrative targets for enemies of U.S. forces operating in cities. Innovative ways to store, conceal, and secure such caches will be called for. Underground facilities such as parking garages (with sufficient overhead clearance for haul vehicles and material-handling equipment operations), warehouses, or stadiums might serve the need. Alternatively, positioning ammunition distribution points in the lee of tall buildings will make it difficult for a foe to hit them with indirect fire from any but a very limited number of points on a compass.

ANTICIPATION AND ADAPTATION

As noted, it is not only the quantities of ammunition that tend to change during urban operations. The mix of ammunition types is also likely to differ considerably from that found in most other environments. Anti-tank sabot rounds for M1 tank and M2 infantry fighting vehicle main armaments have limited utility in a city; they tend to punch cleanly through masonry and other materials, leaving

---

[1]Center for Army Lessons Learned, "Urban Combat Operations: Appendix F: Simple Marking Devices," *http://call.army.mil/products/newsltrs/99-16/appendf.htm,* accessed June 18, 2002. The SBCT requires 5.0 short tons (STONs) per day of ammunition based upon CASCOM-approved planning factors. The ammunition section of the brigade support battalion (BSB) can issue 62 STONs per day, which are about six flat racks. This section can surge to 138 STONs from time to time.

only a small hole in their wake. This ammunition is therefore not well suited for creating dismounted infantry passageways. Additionally, these rounds can travel extensive distances and thereby unnecessarily endanger noncombatants. It has already been noted that the sabots discarded during discharge pose a potentially fatal threat to dismounted forces or civilians in front of the guns. High explosive is better suited for creating passageways through walls, but its tendency to disperse blast laterally rather than forward when striking building materials also makes it less than ideal for "mouse holing." The excessive spalling resulting from such a blast pattern threatens both civilians and friendly force soldiers. The more limited penetration power and reduced lateral blast characteristic of squash head or training rounds make them more effective for opening passageways for dismounts. Such munitions may therefore be requested in greater quantities than is the norm elsewhere. The Multi-purpose, Anti-Tank (MPAT) round being introduced into U.S. armor units in early 2003 has similarly beneficial characteristics. Unfortunately, it is a sabot-type round with the aforementioned hazards for unprotected personnel.

The M908 Multi-purpose, Anti-Tank-Obstacle Reducing (MPAT-OR) round is similar to the M830A1 MPAT 120mm, HEAT-MP-T (high-explosive antitank multipurpose tracer round).[2] One notable difference: the MPAT-OR round has a steel nose in place of the M830A1's RF (radio frequency) proximity switch. The steel nose penetration allows the projectile to penetrate slightly deeper into a target before the warhead explodes. Testing has shown that this additional penetration increases the rubbling capability of the round.

The M908 is especially effective against concrete obstacles, reinforced concrete structures, or walls. It is also effective against cinderblock or brick buildings as well as bunkers and light-armored vehicles.

Both the M908 and M830A1 rounds require a minimum of 200 meters standoff from the expected impact point. Debris from the impact can cause incapacitating or lethal injuries within this distance. Furthermore, the round should not be fired over unprotected

---

[2]Information on the M908 round provided by Albert H. Pomey, Directorate of Training, Doctrine, and Combat Development, Fort Knox, Kentucky, July 31, 2003.

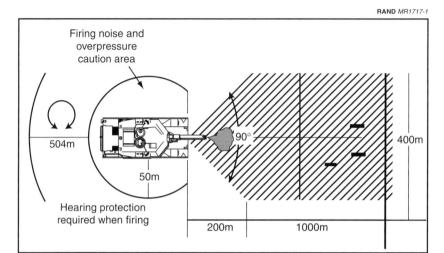

SOURCE: "Abrams Urban Quick Reference Guide," Publication Number ST 3-20.12-1, U.S. Army Training and Doctrine Command, December 2002.

Figure 1—Safety Zone for Unprotected Personnel During the Firing of Sabot Munitions by an Abrams Tank

personnel, due to the risk of the potentially lethal effects of the three discarding aluminum sabots (see Figure 1). The requirements for a 200-meter separation between dismounts and the intended target, and the prohibition against firing unless soldiers and noncombatants are under sufficient cover, diminishes its overall usefulness in urban operations. A similar round with reduced constraints would be especially valuable due to the likelihood that dismounts will frequently be operating with armor vehicles in this environment.

Another desirable adaptation would be a more widespread development and fielding of binary munitions (made of two components that are inert until brought together). Using vehicles to haul materials forward and evacuate wounded on return (a concept discussed later on) could minimize the distance between supply points and medical points would increase CSS efficiency. But such positioning is ill advised at present, since detonation of ammunition would threaten patients and medical personnel. Those dangers would be dramatically reduced were binary weapons adopted, as would similar threats to civilians and others near urban ammunition distribution points. The ability to collocate facilities could also reduce the quantity of resources necessary for maintaining security.

Preservation of innocent life also motivates an increased call for nonlethal weapons, some of which may replace lethal counterparts. The "flash-bang" grenades previously mentioned are already popular alternatives to the fragmentation variety for clearing a building that might contain noncombatants. The nonlethal grenade is first tossed into a room to distract any waiting enemy, with friendly force soldiers following thereafter. Area nonlethal capabilities (e.g., the Area Denial System or ADS) have potential use for controlling crowds during support or stability operations or for isolating areas during combat actions. Such systems induce heat that causes individuals to avoid the affected area. Other nonlethals (for example, slippery foams for road surfaces) will also be entering the inventory either routinely or via special requests. CSS personnel will have to be prepared to transport and supply such items, maintain relevant equipment, and clean up areas when the effects are no longer needed. It is also likely that support units will find it beneficial to employ nonlethal capabilities themselves as they defend storage facilities, protect convoys, or otherwise find a need to influence noncombatant behavior without killing or maiming civilians. Nonlethal development will ideally include means to protect CSS assets and thereby relieve friendly force manpower of that duty (e.g., stationary microwave weapons can be used instead of live guards to deny entry into proscribed areas).

Properly treating those with wounds from nonlethal weapons could require specialized training. The effects could be unfamiliar to medical personnel. An obvious implication is that U.S. medics, physician's assistants (PAs), and doctors need predeployment training in this regard. Similar training ought to be provided to indigenous and coalition member medical personnel. The purposes behind this training are not entirely unselfish. Those on the receiving end of nonlethal capabilities may be wanted by authorities or be sources of valuable information. Finding and interrogating them after a demonstration or disturbance could be beneficial to friendly force intelligence-collection efforts. Such support is likely to be more forthcoming given both the use of nonlethal capabilities and administration of timely medical care.

COMMAND AND CONTROL

CSS leaders should prepare for the second- and higher-order effects these systems will have on operations as nonlethal capabilities enter service inventories. The sequence of vehicles in convoys could be influenced by efforts to most effectively employ such capabilities. Depot, forward area refueling and rearming point (FARP), and other installation site selection could be similarly affected by the new weapons' characteristics. CSS schools should cover such issues in training, just as they should incorporate maintenance, handling, cleanup, and other issues related to the introduction of these nonlethal systems.

Because CSS units will also be primary users of nonlethals, it would benefit support soldiers if their leaders take an active role in development and acquisition. For example, the design of a vehicle-mounted area denial system might focus on its maximum effective range without adequately considering its close-in effectiveness. CSS personnel, having to use the system during convoy escort missions, food distribution operations, or stationary point security, would require the system to deny access to the area immediately around the vehicle as well as more distant locations.

Urban areas present a number of exceptional armament-related CSS requirements. The most fundamental deal with arming the support warriors themselves. It is very likely that CSS missions will result in more frequent and closer contact with noncombatants than is the case for maneuver and combat support units. The opportunities for inadvertently wounding or killing an innocent bystander due to an accidental weapon discharge are therefore also higher. Soldiers experienced with loaded weapons will be far less likely to cause inadvertent discharges. Commanders should consider predeployment garrison training during which their soldiers carry personal weapons loaded with blanks. They could likewise have such rounds chambered in other systems during peacetime exercises. Leaders would then be better able to emphasize the importance of weapons discipline and correct mistakes before they become fatal for fellow soldiers, noncombatants, or the individual in possession of the weapon.

Leaders have a responsibility to ensure that their soldiers are well trained on the implications of employing both nonlethal and lethal systems. This training should go well beyond simple operation of the weapon to encompass:

- Likely reactions by those targeted, including the possibility that they may respond to what they believe is lethal fire

- Inadvertent effects on innocents within the area influenced

- Appropriate ROE for the use of such capabilities

- The legal implications of employing the systems, either by deliberately targeting noncombatants or knowingly including them in the group targeted

- Appropriately task organizing lethal and nonlethal capabilities for soldier protection.

It is notable that the SBCT tactical operations center (TOC) is unique among organizations of its echelon in that it has a nonlethal effects cell (NLEC). This element includes intelligence, civil affairs (CA), and psychological operations (PSYOP) officers as well as enlisted personnel. Its members should be capable of integrating nonlethal use into plans, recommending appropriate pre- and post-deployment training in that regard, recommending stores required for cleanup, and otherwise provide relevant expertise. All are capabilities highly desirable in any unit tasked to conduct operations in built-up areas.

CONCLUDING REMARKS

Anticipation and adaptation with respect to urban arming issues require the CSS soldier to coordinate with his combat and combat support counterparts to determine the munitions needs (both lethal and nonlethal). These requirements include consideration of the consequences of both employing such capabilities and dealing with their aftereffects. With new systems coming on line, the medical training requirements that will affect U.S. forces, coalition members, and the noncombatant community should be identified, and means to communicate them should be developed before any deployments. Such anticipation of needs should occur during the procurement process as well. It is the CSS warrior who will treat the wounded, transport the rounds, maintain the weapon systems, and, probably, be tasked with the responsibility of cleaning up the aftereffects of an operation. It would be wise to take the steps necessary to mitigate unnecessary logistical burdens during the design of such capabilities rather than have to do so in a reactive mode.

Chapter Four

MANNING

> I am proud and honored to have taken care of soldiers injured in combat . . . Unfortunately . . . you do it better the more times you experience it.
>
> Dr. John Holcomb,
> speaking of his service in Mogadishu, Somalia, October 3–4, 1993
> as quoted in *Capital Preservation*

Urban operations are among the most demanding of environments for both personnel managers and commanders. Though the extraordinary casualty rates attributable to urban fighting are well known, a lack of historical data plagues personnel managers and medical people just as it does those dealing with ammunition. There is virtually nothing available in the way of planning factors regarding losses attributable to enemy fire, disease, nonbattle injury, or stress during urban operations.

The physical and mental demands of combat are exhausting regardless of the surroundings, but few others match the intensity of densely populated blocks of manmade structures. For the dismounted soldier, every street and room is a potential enemy engagement area. Every enclosure entered could contain a waiting foe, a booby trap, or innocent civilians huddled in fear. Eyes take dangerous seconds to adjust as a man enters a dark building from a sunlit street. Clearing one story of a structure means that a way must be found to access floors above and below. There are only a limited number of places to do so, and the enemy could be waiting at any or all of them. The combined effect of this constant exposure to danger is rapid, thorough exhaustion. Casualties and exhaustion mean that an urban mission can take two to three times the number of maneuver personnel than would elsewhere be necessary in order to provide needed rest and maintain combat proficiency. Maintaining operational momentum for CSS and maneuver units alike will be a challenge. Maneuver units can compensate by organizing into security, search, and reaction groups. The first isolates search areas and otherwise denies enemy entry into a proscribed area. The search group clears an assigned area, and the reaction team stands by for commitment should either of the other two need support. Combat service support and combat support personnel will be a part of all three. Such task organizing allows a commander to rotate the three groups' responsibilities as one element is drained of its effectiveness. Casualties and the level of stress during urban actions is such that it still may be necessary to replace all three elements more frequently than is elsewhere the norm.

That urban combat is casualty intensive is not news. It may be less widely recognized that a casualty in urban terrain will tend to consume more in the way of personnel, equipment, and evacuation assets. Four stretcher-bearers are the preferred minimum for any casualty, but two can sometimes suffice. Moving urban wounded will often demand navigation of long, twisting routes. Casualties will have to be strapped to stretchers, tipped on their sides, and have one end or the other raised or lowered as they are carried up from basements, through tight mouse holes, or down stairwells. Rare will be the time when two men can handle the burden alone. Longer and tortuous routes mean that evacuations will often take more time. More stretcher-bearers will be needed. Medical leaders will be well advised to consider positioning medical personnel, treatment facilities, evacuation equipment, and related supplies farther forward in the interest of casualty survival.

Meeting these multiple demands for greater numbers of soldiers is especially challenging for organizations that have limited manpower resources or are short of personnel with requisite skills. The durability of these units is also problematic; like others in urban environments, their men and women will quickly suffer exhaustion's attrition. The problem is particularly acute for the Stryker Brigade Combat Team. The SBCT arrives in theater with little hope of receiving substantial numbers of personnel replacements for many days.[1] One analyst noted that "more than any other factor, the lack of a rapid replacement system is the Achilles Heel for the entire [SBCT] and Objective Force Army. Getting into battle in 96 hours is only part of the challenge—the army must be able to stay and fight in even the most intense combat."[2] Just as is the case with any other force committed to an urban involvement, personnel replacement and CSS operational planning needs to account for the likelihood of greater numbers of casualties and rapid exhaustion of service providers.

Operations or campaigns with a significant urban component will demand a force mix tailored to handle the expected variety of tasks and missions such undertakings entail. Until better historical data are developed, proper task organization will unfortunately be a matter of guesswork. For example, just as the data on expected urban loss rates are scarce, so is information pertaining to the likely types of wounds and injuries. There is evidence that certain types of injuries (cuts, abrasions, crush injuries) and wounds (broken bones, bullet strikes to head, arms, and chest) will characterize combat in villages, towns, and cities.[3] The mix of medical specialists deployed for urban

---

[1]"While the Interim and Objective Forces both possess streamlined and substantially more effective methods for casualty evacuation, neither concept addresses the system to replace killed or severely wounded soldiers . . . The '96 Hour Warriors' can get to the battle quickly, and can fight initially, but any losses they take will require weeks to replace even if the support base was mobilized and ready from C-Day [mobilization day] forward." Robert R. Mackey, *Building a Shallow Army: Replacement Operations in the Future Force,* Fort Leavenworth, KS: School of Advanced Military Studies, 2002, p. 17. Mackey also recommends using a form of unit replacement (crews and squads) rather than individual replacement. This has been considered and tested previously. For one of several other discussions of this topic, see Russell W. Glenn, *Reading Athena's Dance Card: Men Against Fire in Vietnam,* Annapolis, MD: Naval Institute Press, 2000.

[2]Mackey, *Building a Shallow Army,* p. 36.

[3]Some discussions of Israeli actions in Lebanon during the early 1980s and operations in Israel proper in the opening years of the 21st century posit that crush injuries due to debris or building collapse, or bullet wounds (due to snipers) will be more common-place during urban operations than elsewhere. Injuries at U.S. urban operations training facilities demonstrate a need for gloves, elbow pads, and kneepads to reduce cuts and impact wounds. On the other hand, John Holcomb noted that wounds suffered by U.S. personnel during October 3–4, 1993, in Mogadishu, Somalia, had "a distribution very similar to any that you see in textbooks regarding war injuries." While the balance of commentary supports a conclusion that urban injuries will differ in character from those elsewhere in many instances, the lack of urban-specific wound and injury data precludes anything more than reporting various empirical

operations should account for such expectations if exercises and actual deployments show them to be justified. Perhaps more orthopedic doctors will be called for, while another specialty's numbers can be sent elsewhere in theater or not deployed at all. This variation in required capabilities will similarly apply to fields other than medical. For example, construction engineers (or contractors with similar skills) capable of repairing electric, water treatment, and other infrastructure will abet both military operational efficiency and a smooth transition of a built-up area to post-operational normalcy.

MEDICAL AND MORTUARY

Adaptation and Anticipation

> The time you get the most casualties is when the first soldier is wounded and others go to his aid . . . . You end up with a pile of wounded.
>
> LTC Harold E. Modrow
> U.S. Army Medical Materiel Development Activity, 2002

Urban operations are especially demanding of those whose mission it is to provide medical attention. It has been noted that the compartmented nature of the urban landscape means that soldiers move in small units. It is not surprising that men go down and are not missed for some time, what with incoming fire plaguing movements, smoke drifting through the area as friendly forces attempt to provide concealment, and obstacles to sight constantly denying leaders vision of their men. Changes, perhaps something as straightforward as creation of a buddy system, can help to mitigate the problem.

The medic is especially vulnerable to enemy fire as he attempts to treat or recover a fallen comrade. Adaptation to the conditions of urban combat seems to suggest a reconsideration of the assumption that immediate aid should be provided to a wounded soldier. In given situations (especially in cases in which the enemy baits his engagement areas by deliberately wounding targets), unwounded and

---

observations. There is a definite and immediate need for an extensive analysis of historical writing to extract reasonable estimates of both personnel and class of supply urban attrition rates.

casualty alike may be better served by allowing a wounded man to treat himself in the short term. Casualty self-treatment is an initial adaptation for getting immediate attention to the wounded, at least when the patient is able to render such self-aid. Cases in which a man is able to do so may be more frequent than might be thought. The increasing use and effectiveness of body armor and the higher quality of helmets means that immobilizing wounds are probably to limbs. Such near-term emerging technologies as the one-handed tourniquet, hemostatic bandage (which dramatically reduces blood loss), or rapid clotting agents will provide those who are conscious and able to use at least one hand the opportunity to stem their own blood loss.[4] Training, including lessons on how to forestall the onset of shock, will be critical to the success of such adaptations. Wounded can subsequently be recovered when the tactical situation has changed sufficiently to allow for safely reaching and removing downed personnel.

This does not imply that alternatives to sending a medic or comrade into a fire-swept street should be ignored. The medical community is developing an individual recovery system in which an immobile soldier automatically propels a line to fellow unit members as they remain behind cover (hopefully in conjunction with the judicious use of smoke to further increase the injured man's opportunity to escape a killing shot). Ad hoc means of recovery and evacuation should also not be overlooked (e.g., using an armored vehicle as a screen, employing smoke, or shining blinding lights toward an enemy at night). Veterans of combat in 1993 Mogadishu offer similar

---

[4]These three developments in particular show excellent near-term promise for use during soldier self-care. The tourniquet is very cheap (approximately $9/unit) and little bigger than what currently fits in the individual first aid pouch carried by every soldier. Hemostatic bandages, made with human plasma-impregnated gauze, are currently extremely expensive (approximately $300 each, though the introduction of artificial plasma could reduce this cost to $50–$100 per unit). Quikclot, essentially a clotting agent packed into a wound, is much cheaper and has proven extremely effective in animal testing. As of early 2003, some U.S. Army and Marine units were purchasing Quikclot. However, reports vary on its effectiveness during the Iraq War of that year. Further testing and development of this and other clotting products is advised. Kathleen M. Sheehan email to Michael J. Leggierir et al., "RE: blast overpressure monitory," June 13, 2002, forwarded to Russell W. Glenn by Sean F. Del Greco, June 14, 2002; Harold E. Modrow telephone interview with Russell W. Glenn, April 9, 2002; "Current News: New Blood-Clotting Material May Revolutionize Combat First Aid," *http://www.mcwl.quantico.usmc.mil/active.html,* accessed July 16, 2002.

advice: "Retrieval of casualties from open areas was often compli-cated by intense small arms fire in Mogadishu. Improved casualty retrieval and area denial methods to include smoke, diversions, custom-made or field-expedient casualty retrieval devices (such as a length of line with a snap link), pursuit deterrent munitions, use of cover, and improved gunfire support plans for the urban environ-ment need to be developed and employed."[5]

It should be noted that this "Soldier, treat thyself" break with tradi-tion is but one consideration motivated by an increasing familiarity with the challenges of urban operations. The reconnaissance com-munity has long argued against wearing anything that made them less quick and stealthy. That marine reconnaissance personnel are recommending to their peers that they don body armor and Kevlar helmets during urban missions reflects how fundamentally different the demands of urban scenarios are.[6] The result of more men wear-ing such equipment could be a reduction of chest and head wounds and a related increase in the percentage of injuries to the extremities, which would, as noted, argue for adjustments in the mix of deployed medical specialists.

A second means of increasing soldier survivability is to move medical care closer to the wounded. The ubiquitous presence of cover in ur-ban areas may in many cases make reducing the distances between areas of fighting and medical aid points a viable policy. "Medical personnel forward" should be consistent guidance for units con-fronting urban combat. Having physician's assistants and doctors nearer the line of contact would reduce the distance the wounded have to travel before they are seen by personnel with more than basic lifesaving skills. The Israelis put doctors on many helicopters, medi-cal evacuation (MEDEVAC) and otherwise, during operations in 1982 Beirut. Casualties among medical personnel were correspondingly high, but the payoff in the improved level of treatment was consid-ered worth the cost.

---

[5]Frank K. Butler and John H. Hagmann (eds.), *Tactical Management of Urban Warfare Casualties in Special Operations,* proceedings from panel conducted by the Special Operations Medical Association, Tampa, FL, December 7, 1998, p. 13.

[6]Russell W. Glenn et al., *Honing the Keys to the City: Refining the United States Marine Corps Reconnaissance Force for Urban Ground Combat Operations,* Santa Monica, CA: RAND, 2003, p. 88.

An American military doctor provides a counter argument to the Israeli view. James Harris, writing of his experiences as a USMC surgeon during the 2003 Iraq War, concluded that "the cabin of a CH-46 [helicopter] is too open and noisy and filled with wind to even check for heart sounds, much less perform advanced surgical procedures."[7] It would appear that further training and consideration of such a policy is called for, as, perhaps, is the development of medical equipment to compensate for the tumultuous conditions inside an aircraft.

Adding to the number of combat lifesavers in units would be another way to increase the quality of care forward. One combat lifesaver per infantry squad is probably no longer sufficient. Similarly, increasing the number of medics is desirable. A potentially very valuable further step would be to upgrade the skills required of these medics. This alternative is contentious because of the additional dollar and training time costs involved in the U.S. Army's recent transition to the more training-intensive military occupational specialty (MOS) 91W level of expertise (roughly analogous to that of a civilian emergency medical technician). Nonetheless, further raising the level of medic expertise to match that of an "independent duty" U.S. Navy corpsman would significantly boost the quality of forward care available to a wounded soldier.[8] Every such enhancement in treatment is potentially lifesaving, given that medical evacuations will be delayed and take longer during urban actions.

---

[7]James Harris, "My Two Wars," *The New York Times,* April 20, 2003, p. 8.

[8]Rating the relative value of training with a head-to-head comparison between the programs for Army medics and Navy corpsmen (who support marines in the field during combat) is difficult. Commander Joseph Cosentino, a Navy doctor, summarized the difference based on his experience as follows: "Army medics (91W) are more focused on field environments and have less clinical experience, versus the standard Navy corpsman [who] has more hospital care experience with greater clinical experience." The greater field emphasis is obviously highly desirable from the combat soldier (or marine) perspective. However, Commander Cosentino goes on to note that "Navy Corpsmen gain greater field experience by going to Fleet Marine Force (FMF) School and becom[ing] 8404's." Such individuals gain sufficient expertise to assume "responsibility of independent duty aboard ships and submarines; Fleet Marine Force, Special Forces and Seabee units, and at isolated duty stations where no medical officer is available." The latter status is the result of a five-year program. While obviously impractical for across-the-board application, similar (combat care oriented) further training would be highly desirable in urban environments where rapid evacuation has frequently proved impossible. Email and accompanying briefing slides from Commander Joseph Cosentino forwarded to Russell W. Glenn, February 6, 2003.

Innovators should not overlook nontraditional applications of available technologies. An interesting adaptation available to medical units without sufficient operational x-ray capabilities is the ad hoc use of EOD (explosive ordnance disposal) scanning equipment to check injuries.[9]

Anticipation and adaptation during concept development and equipment procurement should be as much a part of improving urban capabilities as are battlefield adjustments. NATO doctrine notes that "particular consideration needs to be given to dual voltage implications, different plugs-fittings (in particular for oxygen tubes) and development of standards for stretchers so that they can easily fit in ambulances and MEDEVAC helicopters."[10] Such compatibility of medical equipment between services and nations (and, ideally, PVOs and NGOs) would pay dividends during both crises and routine medical activity.

CSS planners should not overlook the use of indigenous health services in treating U.S. or other coalition member nations' soldiers. These resources are particularly likely to be available in larger cities. An American commander recalled from his Balkan experiences in the 1990s that

> host nation health care support was readily available and the quality was generally on par with U.S. health care. Their laboratory facilities were more sophisticated than the CSH's [Combat Support Hospital's], so we periodically sent laboratory specimens to the Hungarians when they exceeded the capabilities of the CSH . . . A couple of soldiers needed neurosurgical procedures that we could not provide at the CSH. They were surgically treated in the Hungarian medical facility with excellent post-operative results.[11]

---

[9]Russell W. Glenn interview with Special Forces personnel, Tampa, FL, September 19, 2002.

[10]"Improving Land Armaments: Lessons from the Balkans," RTO-TR-AC/323(SAS-041)TP/, Brussels, Belgium: North Atlantic Treaty Organization, November 2001, p. 4.5.2.

[11]William T. Bester, *The Preparation and Deployment of the Initial Medical Force in Support of Operation Joint Endeavor,* Carlisle, PA: United States Army War College, 1998, p. 24.

Nor should anticipation and adaptation be limited to actions within the theater of operations. Variations from wounds received in combat on other terrain will influence the mix of medical specialties brought into a theater. They should also have an impact on the training that medical personnel at every echelon receive before deploying. Just as a maneuver unit trains to conduct its tasks in body armor, medical personnel need to train for the types of wounds expected in a force wearing protective vests. Training should also account for a relative increase in secondary munitions effects (e.g., injuries caused by spalling or falling building materials and concussion injuries due to explosions contained by enclosures) and casualties caused by soldiers stumbling over building debris. Training medics and engineers on how to properly remove rubble that has fallen on a man so as not to increase the extent of his injuries is essential, as is recognizing the symptoms of internal injuries due to crushing or compression. These may be the result of impact by falling materials, overpressure from weapons in the increasingly commonplace thermobaric family of munitions, or the just mentioned pressure resulting from large-caliber weapons firing in enclosed or semi-enclosed areas.

Thermobaric weapons are among those that might be seen more frequently in built-up areas due to their greater effectiveness there. These systems are particularly destructive when their effects are contained. They can cause burns or fragmentation wounds, but the primary damage is inflicted on internal organs due to overpressure that can leave virtually no external sign of injury. Symptoms of an attack can include deafness (difficult to gauge if the victim is unconscious) and fluid in the ears of some (but not all) victims. Missing the symptoms of possible overpressure injury can result in treatment that exacerbates existing damage. Medical training should include advising personnel to look at the area around the wounded soldier for telltale signs of a thermobaric attack. On the other hand, factors such as whether the patient has moved or been moved from the original place of injury might not be immediately evident to those providing aid.[12] Medical personnel should ask conscious patients for

---

[12]Guidance on treatment for thermobaric injuries differs even within the U.S. Army medical community, probably a function of inexperience with treating such casualties. Dr. Lee Cancio extrapolates from his experience with blunt trauma and burn injuries

pertinent information or query others in the area when possible. Training for treating suspected overpressure victims should include the following guidance:

- Introduce intravenous lines (IVs) with caution. The introduction of fluid can worsen a casualty's condition due to lung damage incurred during the attack. However, injury to the spleen and other organs is likely to require the infusion of these same fluids.

- Be prepared to provide ventilatory support forward on the battlefield and to do so within six to eight hours of injury.

- The condition of the patient will most likely mean that medical evacuation by the fastest feasible means is desirable. However, damage to lungs—and the possibility that the changes in atmospheric pressure experienced during air evacuation might exacerbate that damage—could call for alternative means of evacuation from medical points in the rear. In such cases, it is advisable not to air evacuate without preparing the patient for life-threatening problems en route (barotrauma).

---

when providing his cautions regarding "fluid resuscitation" (use of IVs). IVs can cause lung failure in blunt trauma patients within a one to twenty hour timeframe after injury. The danger is that the medic will attempt to rapidly "push" two bags of IV fluid and cause lung failure. However, Dr. Cancio also cautions that one cannot "run these patients dry," as other injuries will worsen should fluids not be provided. The critical factor seems to be the rate at which the fluid is introduced into the patient. Too rapid fluid resuscitation risks lung failure. Too slow (or too little) risks failure of other organs. He recommends treating thermobaric casualties (or suspected thermobaric casualties) in a manner similar to burn patients or any other severely injured soldier: Begin by opening the airway and stopping compressible hemorrhaging as necessary. Introduce an IV if the patient is suffering from a systolic blood pressure of 90 or less and has a palpable radial pulse and intact mental status. If there is no palpable radial pulse, check for a coradic pulse. If the coradic pulse is present, introduce an IV and vigorously resuscitate, thereafter cutting the IV rate to maintain a normal pulse rate and blood pressure.

With regard to air evacuation, Dr. Cancio recommends using the method if it is available; the likely severe state of injury may well make the risk of further lung damage acceptable. If the evacuation is from a more rearward medical treatment facility, however, the means of evacuation should depend on the PA's or doctor's best judgment. If a lung puncture is known or thought to exist, use air evacuation only if it is thought clinically feasible, as blow out is a major concern in such cases. LTC Lee Cancio telephone interview by Russell W. Glenn, February 12, 2003. It is obvious that further research and discussion of proper treatment methods is highly desirable given that such advice is based on other injury types.

- Do not consider the casualty a "walking wounded" even if he is initially able to walk.

- Examine the eardrums (Note, however, that field medics currently have no means to do so other than looking at the exterior of the ear).

The medical consequences of operating in urban areas go beyond those related to increases in the numbers and variety of wounds. The extreme physiological and mental demands will require physical training before, changes in support during, and a readiness to address consequences after actions. For example, both the Russians and U.S. Marines recognize the need to increase caloric intake during urban operations. In Grozny, Chechnya, the Russians found themselves unable to meet their goal of 150 percent of normal calorie levels due to losses suffered by soft-skinned logistics vehicles and inadequately designed dry rations. Both are problems that could similarly interfere with future U.S. feeding efforts.[13]

Longer-term adaptations should include consideration of technological means of mitigating urban-related injuries. Perhaps the development of body armor with plates that interlock when subjected to sudden pressures (thereby forming a solid shell that protects the wearer's torso, neck, and head during a thermobaric or similar attack) would increase chances of soldier survival. Possibly the body armor currently being developed at the Natick Soldier Center (which has a standoff between the chest and back areas of the body) will help in this regard.[14] It might be that the nature of thermobaric injuries is such that damage to unprotected body parts (legs, arms, and groin) would result in fatalities even were such armor worn. Such issues should be addressed during ongoing efforts to improve body

---

[13]While the U.S. Army's dietary guidelines do not address urban needs specifically, they do recognize that "military personnel doing heavy work or involved in prolonged, vigorous physical training may have energy requirements that exceed 125 percent of the [Military Dietary Reference Intakes] for energy (for example, 4000 to 5000 calories/day)." Army Regulation 40-25, "Nutrition Standards and Education," Washington, D.C.: Headquarters, Departments of the Army, Navy, and Air Force, June 15, 2001, p. 4.

[14]"Objective Force Warrior: Soldiers On Point For The Nation," brochure published by the Natick Soldier Center, Natick, MA, undated; and Jean-Lewis DeGay interview with Russell W. Glenn, Natick, MA, May 2, 2003.

armor, face protection, vehicle survivability, and other relevant initiatives.

The medical treatment and force protection considerations of dealing with thermobaric injury considered immediately above are but two factors influencing soldiers' urban survival. A systemic approach to this threat would consider not only personal body armor and medical treatment, but also weapon effects mitigation procedures such as:

- Constructing a series of standoff protective measures, including wire mesh ("chicken wire") put in front of positions to interdict incoming rounds and cause premature detonation.

- Suspending barriers such as wet fabric or Kevlar "blast blankets" across doorways and/or windows to further disrupt incoming rounds and the distribution of overpressure effects within a structure.

These two practices are presented purely for exemplary purposes; neither approach has (to the authors' knowledge) yet been tested for effectiveness. Both, however, are among what should be a broad spectrum of possible solutions that breach the boundaries of functional areas and bureaucratic organizations.

Other developments in medical doctrine, training, or technology worthy of consideration in preparation for future CSS urban operations include:

- Designating vehicles for multiple uses, e.g., vehicles employed for hauling materials forward might be designated as ambulances or used to transport remains on return trips. While such a procedure is within the constraints of international law, there are obvious practical risks inherent in such a practice.[15] An enemy

---

[15]Regarding international wars, the "Protocol Additional to the Geneva Conventions of 12 August 1949, and relating to the protection of victims of international armed conflicts (Protocol I)" clarifies and expands on protections from previous conventions. Relevant to the discussion here, this document states that

"Medical transports" means any means of transportation, whether military or civilian, permanent or temporary, assigned exclusively to medical transportation and under the control of a competent authority of a Party to the conflict [Article 8 (7)]. Further,

knowing that his adversary uses ammunition trucks to haul wounded during retrograde movements might find it difficult not to destroy those vehicles as they move en route to a hospital even were they properly displaying a red cross. Sparing mechanized or armored fighting vehicles used for evacuation would take even greater restraint. Further, care would have to be exercised were vehicles to be used for such varied purposes. For health reasons—perhaps even more importantly for psychological reasons—vehicles used to evacuate wounded or remains should arguably not subsequently be tasked to transport Class I (foodstuffs).

• Fitting selected dual-purpose vehicles with portable trauma centers would be an extension of this concept. Being able to quickly retrofit one or more vehicle chassis types with a compact "mini aid station" would give medical leaders greater flexibility than having to rely on a lesser number of ambulances. Medics, physician's assistants, or doctors could move forward with a convoy, either in the specially equipped vehicles (at that point hauling other than medical supplies) or in others marked with medical symbols to identify them as care providers.

"temporary medical transports" mean those devoted exclusively to medical purposes for limited periods during the whole of such periods. Unless otherwise specified, the terms "medical personnel," "medical units" and "medical transports" cover both permanent and temporary categories. (Article 8 (11), *http://fletcher.tufts.edu/multi/texts/ BH707.txt*; accessed October 21, 2002.)

In the case of noninternational conflict, the "Protocol Additional to the Geneva Conventions of 12 August 1949, and relating to the Protection of Victims of Non-International Armed Conflicts (Protocol II), 8 June 1977. Part III: Wounded, sick and shipwrecked" reads as follows:

4712. The term "medical transports" means any land vehicle (cars, trucks, trains etc.), ship, craft or aircraft assigned to transporting the wounded, sick and shipwrecked, medical and religious personnel, and medical equipment. Protection applies for military and civilian medical units and transports, whether they are permanent or temporary, provided that they are exclusively assigned to medical purposes; while they are so assigned, whether or not for an indefinite period, depending on whether they are permanent or temporary, medical units and transports may not be used for any purposes other than medical ones. The concept "medical purposes" should be understood in a broad sense. It covers not only the care given the wounded, sick and shipwrecked, but also any activities for the prevention of disease, blood transfusion centres, rehabilitation centres for medical treatment and dental treatment. *(http://www.icrc.org/ihl.nsf/1a13044f3bbb5b8ec12563fb0066f226/edb39a930fd78699c125 63cd0043a86d?OpenDocument*, accessed October 22, 2002.)

- Robotic casualty evacuation is currently not available. However, unmanned vehicles of sufficient size to transport wounded or dead could soon be commonplace on the battlefield. Whether equipped to pick up human beings mechanically or simply to move to an exposed location where semi-ambulatory wounded climb aboard, such a capability would potentially save lives of wounded, preclude further losses of combatants who might otherwise try to recover downed comrades, and preserve the combat power lost when using stretchers. These vehicles, like their manned counterparts discussed above, could be ambulances or have that function as one of many tasks for which they are used.

- The prescribed use of performance-enhancing drugs is not unknown in the military world. The physical and mental exertion that typifies urban operations suggests that they might be of value during such contingencies. Future developments could seek to address specific challenges likely to confront the urban warrior (e.g., by reducing or eliminating the need for sleep for extended periods, making soldiers stronger, reducing food and water requirements, or decreasing susceptibility to stress, shock, or bleeding out). They would preferably be administered in a form not requiring medical personnel or sanitizing (e.g., pills or skin patches impregnated with antibiotics would be preferable to injections). Doctors are already working with an experimental technique involving what are called "nutraceuticals," chemicals that would trick a soldier's brain into thinking his stomach is full or his muscles are not really tired, significantly (if temporarily) improving soldier stamina during urban combat.[16] Walter Reed Army Research Institute is exploring the use of caffeinated chewing gum called "Stay Alert" for use by fatigued soldiers on patrol or to combat jet lag after long-distance deployments. Two of these sticks equal the equivalent of a cup of coffee. Research so far shows the gum causing quicker body responses than the

---

[16]Scripps New Service, "Hold the Lettuce: Nutrition Patches in Soldiers' Future," *http://www.thedailycamera.com/science/20apatc.html*. Article provided by Jerry Darsch, Department of Defense Combat Feeding Program, Natick Soldiers Systems Center, Natick, Massachusetts.

same amount of caffeine in a beverage.[17] While these capabilities will not be available for several years, a currently fielded item is the "HooAH! Bar," a food bar akin to popular energy bars that provide approximately 250 calories each.[18] A version of the bar containing the equivalent of six cups of coffee was developed for physiological testing only. Up to the equivalent of 1.5 cups of coffee can be incorporated into the bar "depending on military requirements for a caffeine product."[19]

- Capitalizing on the development of artificial plasma to reduce the cost of hemostatic bandages, or the general distribution of a proven artificial coagulant in individual first aid packets.

- Protection for the groin, face, neck, and extremities similar to that currently available for the torso and head.[20]

- Soldier location monitors would assist in finding missing men, to include those wounded during movements through urban areas. Status monitors would at a minimum tell leaders and medical personnel whether a casualty was alive or not. It would preferably send vital signs and perhaps a preliminary diagnosis of injuries and how imminently treatment is necessary for survival. To avoid excessive bandwidth use or signal emissions, the status monitor could be remotely activated when a soldier is found to be missing, when querying a unit to establish its status (e.g., exhaustion levels), or only at short range to determine a casualty's status and determine whether immediate recovery should be undertaken.

Command and Control

The aforementioned large numbers of casualties, limited quantities of medical personnel and supplies, and the battlefield obstacles likely to separate aid providers from the wounded are but a sampling

---

[17]Jerry Darsch, Department of Defense Combat Feeding Program, Natick Soldiers Systems Center, Natick, Massachusetts, telephone interview with Steven L. Hartman, October 4, 2002.

[18]Ibid.

[19] Email from Jack Briggs to Russell W. Glenn, Subject: HOOAH! Bar, May 20, 2003.

[20]Work in this area is ongoing. DeGay interview.

of the issues that will make management of medical resources a significant challenge. NATO doctrine recommends equipping medical command vehicles with two radios, putting a radio in every ambulance, ensuring that they are capable of secure communications, providing the medical community with GPS, and manning these organizations with sufficient communications personnel to sustain these systems during urban operations.[21] Representatives participating in the March 2001 USMC Project Metropolis experimentation unsurprisingly found that providing more medical personnel with radios increased responsiveness. Unfortunately, their radio traffic threatened to overload the administration and logistics (A&L) net, and the radios were not capable of secure communications. Alternatives to increasing the number of radios, communicating in the clear, and burdening admin and logistics nets need to be found. Allocating medical unit-specific frequencies and use of code words to communicate requirements might be part of a larger solution set.

Preventive medicine is notably important during urban operations, and it remains as much a leader responsibility then as elsewhere. Water, notably potable water, may be in short supply. Water and food found locally could be poisoned or otherwise contaminated. Diseases such as hepatitis, diarrhea, and others causing abdominal problems ravaged Russian forces in Grozny due to poor leadership and wanting soldier discipline. The age-old problem of having soldiers wash their hands before eating is more difficult when clean water is in short supply. Substituting disposable moisturized towels may be a temporary substitute. Preventive medicine is no less significant as a priority when offering aid to the local population.[22] So doing has the added benefit of possibly reducing the chances that friendly force personnel are exposed to preventable diseases.

Heat injuries pose a danger during urban operations just as they do elsewhere. After Operation Just Cause in 1989 in Panama City, soldiers recommended that combat lifesavers be trained to administer

---

[21]"Improving Land Armaments: Lessons from the Balkans," pp. 3.1.36, 4.1.2, 4.4.6, 4.5.1, and 4.5.3.

[22]Ritchie and Mott, "Caring for Civilians during Peace Keeping Missions," p. 15.

IV fluids to prevent debilitating heat injuries.[23] The risk of stress casualties has already been highlighted. Proper training, early identification of symptoms, and effective treatment can all positively influence the numbers and extent of stress casualties, yet too rarely are steps taken to prevent or mitigate their effects.

Urban terrain management puts special demands on leaders. While buildings provide excellent concealment and often offer sufficient cover, locations well suited to all requirements of particular CSS functions (e.g., access to water, easy access and egress, line-of-sight for communications, easy to secure) will be rare. They will therefore be coveted by many. CSS managers need to designate which units have priority for site selection and thereafter manage urban terrain assets no less stringently than they have done in more open terrain. Aid station locations should be given a high priority. Medical needs for access to water and helicopter landing zones (LZs) outweigh most other CSS functions in importance.[24] Reconnaissance forces and CSS soldiers whose jobs allow them to see much of an area of operations need to know how to identify and report sightings of urban sites that meet aid station, hospital, and other provider needs.

Preparing for Extraordinary Challenges

There are a number of other problems with which urban areas burden the medical community. Increased densities of friendly forces means that larger numbers of coalition nations will be in close proximity, and they will sometimes lack the quality of medical care that is available to Americans. Policies regarding the extent to which U.S. medical facilities will provide either routine or emergency care for allies need to be determined and made known early during operations to preclude avoidable negative repercussions and unrealistic expectations. The same is true of the degree to which noncombatant support will be provided. Joint doctrine reminds readers that "diseases behave differently in urban areas due to the high concentration of people. Any disruption in basic services increases the

---

[23]*Operation Just Cause Lessons Learned: Volume III—Intelligence, Logistics, & Equipment,* Fort Leavenworth, KS: U.S. Army Center for Lessons Learned, October 1990, no page numbers.

[24]Ibid.

threat from high-risk diseases such as human immunodeficiency virus (HIV), cholera, tuberculosis, dengue, and malaria."[25] Interruptions in routine medical care due to war or other forms of instability can have dramatic effects on an urban population's health. Providing medical treatment to civilians, or facilitating that treatment by indigenous or PVO/NGO providers, could influence perceptions of mission success, save local noncombatants' lives, and reduce the chances of disease spread to U.S. personnel.

It may be that U.S. medical personnel obtain training benefits when helping other than their own personnel. Army dental assets were underutilized during U.S. force deployments to Somalia in the 1990s. The commander of the 46th Forward Support Battalion, 10th Mountain Division (Light Infantry), Lieutenant Colonel Jack L. Weiss, recalled that "we opened the door for dental sick call to many coalition units which did not have dental support . . . Our doctors began working with Tunisian doctors by providing medical services to Somali children at what became known as the Tunisian Children's Clinic."[26] Such aid is a potentially powerful implement. Properly wielded, its potential benefits for U.S. units include enhanced security and intelligence collection via the indigenous population's greater willingness to interact with U.S. personnel. These effects should not be left to happenstance. They should instead be part of a conscious campaign that coordinates them with other forms of civil affairs, PSYOP, and additional types of suasion in the service of identified friendly force objectives. Such a campaign would have to include consideration of how to avoid the negative consequences of the inevitable reduction or curtailing of such assistance. Doctrine reminds medical providers that "restrictions may be necessary because of a shortage of medical supplies, cultural considerations, financial or legal constraints, or an attempt to keep the level of care consistent with that normally provided by local health services."[27] Providing care without considering the longer-term consequences

---

[25]*Urban Operations, FM 3-06 (90-10)* (Drag edition), Washington, D.C.: Headquarters, Department of the Army, May 20, 2002, p. IV-11.

[26]Jack L. Weiss, *Personal Experience Monograph: Supporting the Quick Reaction Force in Somalia—Operation Continue Hope/Somalia, July 1993–February 1994,* Carlisle, PA: United States Army War College, 1996, p. 32.

[27]*Doctrine for Joint Urban Operations,* Joint Publication 3-06, Washington, D.C., Office of the Joint Chiefs of Staff, September 16, 2002, p. IV-11.

could result in far greater disadvantages than benefits. As with any action in an urban area, second- and higher-order effects have to be a part of planning and execution.

Those who establish programs for treating civilians also need to be cognizant of potential problems with local social norms. A vignette from American history demonstrates a point no less pertinent in some areas of the world today. Forward thinkers of the past proposed a program of mass smallpox vaccinations for colonial Americans, but "controversy attended inoculation from the start. When Cotton Mather supported Dr. Zabdiel Boylston's experiments in Boston in 1721, the result was uproar and shock. Was it not, asked one minister, 'a distrust of God's overruling care' to inoculate? Dr. William Douglas (who later had a change of heart) reckoned it a sin 'to propagate infection by this means.' The furor culminated in the firebombing of Mather's house on November 13, 1721."[28] American medical personnel's unwitting violation of local taboos could precipitate similarly passionate responses with negative consequences for U.S. objectives.

The handling of civilian dead demands a similar need for sensitivity to indigenous cultural norms. Governmental authorities, family, other native representatives, or those from PVOs or NGOs should be relied on to recover remains to as great an extent as possible. Given the concentration of civilians in urban areas, however, and the potential for very large number of deaths due to combat action, disease, or other causes, it may be necessary for U.S. military personnel to assist in the movement, burial, or other handling of the dead. It will be important that the procedures followed are in accordance with local religious and social practices, both of which should be determined prior to the initiation of recovery operations whenever possible.[29] Further, such tasks will require access to body bags, masks, and gloves for soldiers. Soldiers will require training to ensure that their actions are in accordance with local expectations, that their own health is not endangered, and that they not suffer undue psy-

---

[28]Elizabeth A. Fenn, *Pox Americana: The Great Smallpox Epidemic of 1775–82*, New York: Hill and Wang, 2001, p. 36.

[29]"Chaplains advise commanders on matters of religion as it affects the soldiers within their units. They also explain the influences of local religions on the urban populace and their potential effects on Army forces and UO" (FM 3-06, p. 9-24).

chological problems. The latter can be mitigated through diligent preparation, monitoring, and (as necessary) treatment. The following guidance was disseminated during operations in Somalia:

> Mortuary affairs support for Somali nationals is limited to transfer of remains to the nearest township to be turned over to a hospital, family member, or any [official] willing to accept remains. If circumstances preclude transporting or transfer of remains to local officials for burial then remains should be shrouded with a suitable material and buried with all personal effects . . . A statement of incident is required for the Mortuary Affairs Officer (MAO) as soon as possible after the incident.[30]

The historical casualty costs of urban combat call the Army's capabilities to handle its own dead into question as well. The Army has but one active duty and two reserve mortuary affairs companies. Extended combat in a major urban area could strain a command's resources even if all three were serving in a single area of operations. Refining standing operating procedures and developing doctrine for the rapid training of soldiers to temporarily assume mortuary responsibilities would be a wise precaution.

LEGAL

> The limits of authority of commanders at all levels over civilian government officials and the civilian population must be established and understood. A commander must have that degree of authority necessary to accomplish his mission. However, the host government's responsibility for its populace and territory can affect the commander's authority in civil-military matters.
>
> FM 3.06.11, *Combined Arms Operations in Urban Terrain*

The demands on military legal advisors working in densely populated areas differ in both scope and character from those elsewhere. The quotation above reveals the tensions that lawyers and commanders will have to deal with, but fails to fully recognize the extent of the

---

[30]COL Stephen P. Hayward, *Personal Experience Monograph, DISCOM S-3, Somalia (29 Dec 92–25 Feb 93),* Carlisle Barracks, PA: U.S. Army War College, 1998, enclosure "Memorandum for Cdr, 210th FSB, ATTN: SSG Wynn. Subject: Mortuary Affairs Collection Point MTOE," HQ, 10th DISCOM, 19 January 1993.

challenge. Commanders and those advising them will frequently find that "the host government" does not consist of a single entity or representative. The same tiers of urban government that one finds in the United States have parallels around the world. A force operating within the confines of a major city should not be surprised to find itself dealing with the equivalent of U.S. neighborhood representatives, city government, county officials, and state authorities in addition to those with national responsibilities, all within the confines of a single area of operations due to the density of an urban environment. Within a given echelon, e.g., city government, multiple agencies such as police, fire, city council, and the mayor's office will wield influence, with the measure of that influence depending on the metropolitan area, personalities, issue of concern, and myriad other matters. It will be the military lawyers' responsibility to sort through these many actors and determine the impact of each on a commander's authority and international legal standards.

American soldiers will have to know how to handle matters related to civilian labor, the protection of noncombatants, the division of authority between local police and themselves, acceptable reactions to criminal activities involving local civilians, and many other issues. Members of the local population and media representatives will scrutinize Americans' actions. U.S. urban doctrine provides a sampling of the variety of challenges its military representatives are likely to confront during urban operations overseas. Soldiers will have to know how to handle matters related to:

- **Forced labor.** "The Geneva Accords prohibit the use of civilians in combat. However, they may be used before the battle reaches the city. Commanders will be given guidelines for use of civilian labor . . . The brigade or battalion TF may force civilians over 18 years of age to work if the work does not oblige them to take part in military operations. Permitted jobs include maintenance of public utilities as long as those utilities are not used in the general conduct of the war."[31]

- **Civilian resistance groups.** "Units may encounter civilian resistance groups whose actions may range from lending supplies,

---

[31]*Combat Service Support,* Field Manual 3-06.11, Chapter 13, *http://155.217.58/cgi-bin/atdl.dll/fm/3-06.11/ch13.htm,* p. 13-34.

services, and noncombat support to the enemy to actively fighting against friendly forces. Members of such resistance groups
should be dealt with in accordance with applicable provisions of
the law of war."[32]

- **Accompanying civilians.** "Civilians who are accompanying their
  armed forces with an identity card authorizing them to do so are
  treated as enemy prisoners of war (EPWs). For example, when
  captured; civilian members of military aircraft crews, war corre-
  spondents, supply contractors, and members of labor units or
  service organizations responsible for the welfare of the armed
  forces."[33]

Lawyers will be further challenged to define what is permissible so as
not to unnecessarily constrain U.S. forces in their pursuit of mission
accomplishment. They will have the responsibility to assist leaders
in training soldiers who will have to distinguish between legitimate
and illicit targets in the frenzy of combat. Those soldiers will need to
know *before* they go into action when it is acceptable for them to fire
on targets that are intermingled with civilians. Legal advisors can
assist in developing training and rehearsals involving such difficult
circumstances, preparations that will hopefully save Americans from
the moment's hesitation that could cost them their lives. The close
proximity of PVOs, NGOs, media, and other civilians means that Staff
Judge Advocate personnel will have to advise commanders on the extent to which members of such groups fall under the authority of
military leaders in various circumstances. More than in any other
environment, the advice proffered by military legal experts will have
a direct impact on the survival and welfare of Americans, indigenous
personnel, and representatives of organizations from around the
world.

FINANCE AND CONTRACTING

Finance and contracting considerations will differ less in character
than in scope when operations have a significant urban element. If
the situation is such that the urban infrastructure is still operational,

---

[32]Ibid.

[33]Ibid., p. 13-35. Additional coverage of legal issues appears pp. 13-34 to 13-36.

contracting for water, electricity, and similar support can dramatically reduce the burden on supply lines. Similarly, contracting for indigenous vehicle support, labor, and other necessities can (and should) influence the quantities and types of materiel and personnel brought into the theater, further reducing the burden and perhaps allowing other mission-critical assets to arrive sooner than would otherwise have been possible.

Previous contracting efforts in urban areas have left valuable lessons learned on the need for greater coordination between coalition members, PVOs, NGOs, and commercial interests. During UN operations in Mogadishu, a routine rotation of the forces in a particular area of operations led to the replacement of a better-financed military unit by one from a less well-to-do country. The replacement leadership could not afford to pay the same rates for indigenous services, arousing considerable ill will among the native population. Similar shortfalls could also result in reduced situational awareness, as HUMINT reporting previously fueled by generous funding would presumably fall off dramatically. Other theaters have seen PVOs or NGOs inadvertently inflate local urban prices with payments for security, vehicles, or other assistance. Urban areas are especially susceptible to such inflation due to the close proximity of forces and the resulting ability of indigenous merchants to readily find alternative customers for their services (or to play one off another). Coalition leaders should work with member nation militaries and, ideally, private and nongovernmental representatives and commercial interests (to include U.S. contractors) to fix prices or otherwise address the negative effects of price wars and disruption of the local economy. Such discussions would have to include consideration of the currencies used for payment, standards for barter exchanges, and the destabilizing effects of hyperinflation on an economy that should benefit rather than be undermined by outside organizations' presence during an operation. Steps to limit individual soldier spending may be desirable for the same reason. Encouraging and facilitating a reduction in the percentage of pay actually taken in hand during operations or the use of script are but two ways that finance authorities could assist in maintaining a stable local economy. The benefits of such actions need to be balanced with an understanding of the longer-term effects. Creation of the Arizona Market (an area of entrepreneurial trade that sprang up on safe, neutral ground protected by peacekeeping forces) in northern Bosnia-Herzegovina had very positive short-term effects, but the market later became a center for black marketing and other crime. As is the case with any military operation, economic initiatives should be planned, wargamed, and controlled for as long as necessary to achieve the desired end state.

Chapter Five

SUSTAINING AND MOVING

Schilling felt disbelief, and now some guilt. He had steered the convoy the wrong way . . . Over and over he muttered, "We're going to keep driving around until we're all . . . dead."

Mark Bowden, *Black Hawk Down,*
on fighting in 1993 Mogadishu, Somalia

The challenges surrounding urban sustainment and movement are integrally connected. While there are unquestionably elements that fall into either one functional area or the other without significant overlap, the authors found that considering the challenges associated with the two were more effectively presented together.

It is important to note that the initial provisioning and continuing replenishment of a force participating in urban operations need not occur within the confines of the built-up area itself. Army doctrine reminds us that reconnaissance units are to be "resupplied prior to entering the urban area," presumably because it can be done well behind the line of contact and reduces the risk of compromising the unit's mission.[1]   The doctrine envisions these "soldier top-off points" as being applicable primarily at battalion or brigade level. The services provided there can be as detailed as assets and time permit; they are normally provided in a relatively secure location such as a lodgment area, the brigade support area, or the combat

---

[1] *RSTA Squadron,* Field Manual 3-20.96 (2nd Coordinating Draft), U.S Army Armor Center, June 12, 2001, p. 7-17; FM 3-06.11, p. 13-11.

trains. When the mission involves a *coup de main*, it also helps to avoid loss of momentum and ensures that the force is at peak logistical status for the action.[2] Observations from urban warfare experiments conducted by the Marine Corps Warfighting Laboratory (MCWL) note that one way of speeding resupply, whether at top-off points or farther forward, is to preload magazines on ships or in rear areas rather than having the task done by forward field deployed CSS elements. Marine Corps literature reports that "this may require periodic augmentation by available [personnel] from non-CSS units or contract labor if security conditions can be met."[3]

Use of these "soldier top-off points" is in keeping with the split-basing concept that involves "locating assets in the rear and forward with all but the immediate essential held in the rear."[4] The objective is to provide just-in-time tailored support to U.S. units while minimizing the size of their footprint in the AO (thereby reducing their vulnerability). Materials are pushed forward as needed whenever and wherever feasible. More mobile CSS assets are prepositioned to enter the area of operations in a manner most responsive to potential fighting force demands. Intermediate supply bases are a form of split basing. Such points, which could include one or more top-off points, are

> usually established within the theater of operations near to, but not in, the AO. While not a requirement, an intermediate support base (ISB), or multiple ISBs if required, may provide a secure, high-throughput facility when circumstances warrant . . . The ISB may

---

[2]Colonel Larry Harman sees "logistics replenishment [as] *a quick, on-the-fly, sustainment operations that fits within the battle rhythm.* This is similar to a 'pit stop' operation," and it would be so in this case. Larry Harman, *Objective Force White Paper: The Expeditionary Support Force (ESF) and Maneuver Sustainment Support (MSS)*, Fort Lee, VA: CASCOM CSS Battle Lab, November 11, 2001, p. 37 (emphasis in original). A *coup de main* would be an operation in which an attacker storms into a built-up area in an effort to overwhelm any defenders via shock and, as necessary, firepower in contrast to a deliberate attack. It could also refer to an operation in which the attacker suddenly surrounds all or part of an urban area in the same manner to achieve a similar effect.

[3]"Urban Sustainability," X-File 3-35.12, Quantico, VA: Marine Corps Warfighting Laboratory (MCWL), June 25, 1999, p. 7.

[4]*The Interim Brigade Combat Team*, FM 3-21.31 (7-32) (Draft), Fort Benning, GA: United States Army, July 10, 2001, p. 10-2. The concept could of course apply to any class of supply or service.

also be referred to as "sanctuary." . . . There are two basic roles for an
ISB: as staging bases for deploying units in transit to an AO and as a
remote support base . . . Aspects of such functions as distribution
management, materiel management, and some personnel or legal
functions may be performed by elements at an ISB.[5]

In the case of urban operations, such points might well be in the area
of operations but either outside of the built-up area or in a secure
portion thereof.

Support for virtually any unit type can employ split basing to some
extent. The 96-hour objective for deploying the SBCT, for example,
means that the concept will be an integral part of its operations, at
least initially upon its arrival in a theater. SBCT doctrine bases its
sustainment procedures on several assumptions. It is expected that
the brigade will deploy with 72 hours of supply carried on organic
vehicles. Beyond that period, sustainment packages will be delivered
in tailored unit-configured loads by echelons above brigade (EAB)
organizations. Refueling and water operations will normally occur
every other day and be provided from prepositioned stocks or via
host nation contracts, both of which are the responsibility of the Defense Logistics Agency (DLA). Meals Ready to Eat (MRE) (or replacements under development) will be the only food source until
food service augmentation arrives in theater.

Current doctrinal thinking on force sustainment seeks to maximize
efficiency and responsiveness to warfighter needs regardless of the
operating environment or unit TOE. The intent is to create a
seamless distribution-based CSS structure from the factory floor to
the soldier in the field. Making this concept viable requires an agile
force with a reasonable logistical signature that can reliably deliver
just the right amount of sustainment to the customer at the right
time. To accomplish this requires complete source-to-customer situational understanding as sustainment materials flow through the
system.

Configured loads will be an essential element of this distribution-
based system. The authors of Field Manual 3-20.96 discuss three
types of configured loads: strategic, mission, and unit, involving

---

[5]Ibid., pp. 10-3 to 10-5.

concepts conceivably applicable to any type of operation or unit force structure. Strategic configured loads (SCL) are those assembled outside of the theater of operations (most likely within the sanctuary of the United States) with the intent of minimizing the logistical footprint. The doctrine stipulates that these loads be built for specific unit types based on a standard requirements code (SRC) without regard for the mission at hand. Ongoing sustainment using this type of load would be consolidated through the requisite Supply Support Activity (SSA). A shortcoming is that there would be little flexibility in influencing SCL contents. The intent is to offer a reasonable level of consumer satisfaction over extended periods based on a fixed interval of delivery. Mission Configured Loads (MCL) offer the same characteristics as SCL except that they are built inside the theater of operations for a specific mission, unit, or purpose. These loads would be configured at theater or corps level, most likely at an intermediate support base. A Unit Configured Load (UCL) is usually built forward of the corps to meet consuming unit specifications. UCL, traditionally called logistics packages (LOGPACs), are targeted at squadron and battalion level sustainment.[6]

This doctrinal concept of configured loads might be too inflexible to meet the demands of urban combat. It has been noted that such fighting will involve small units engaged in high-intensity combat for extended periods while dispersed over a sizable and highly compartmented area. The current LOGPACs for a battalion or squadron-sized unit do not offer sufficient flexibility to such contingencies. SCL, and probably MCL as well, are unlikely to account for demands such as those due to the intensive consumption of small arms Class V ammunition that is characteristic of urban combat. Truly responsive configurations will also have to consider nonlethal munitions as part of sustainment planning. Urban-tailored loads and a refinement of the proposed doctrine are two means of addressing these shortfalls.

---

[6]The U.S. Army is getting ready to distribute a battlebook for configured loads at the time of this document's publication. Essentially, these loads will be broken into four segments: mission, unit, capability, and commodity. A mission-configured load is a generic package of supplies; a unit-configured load will be a specifically tailored mission configuration for a particular unit. A capability module will be a smaller subset of the mission or unit configured load for support of small teams or squads. A commodity module will include materials configured around a certain class of supply. CASCOM, DCD-QM telephone interview with Steven Hartman, March 6, 2003.

Urban SCL would conceivably address both the high levels of urban consumption and the nature of its typical task organizations. Urban operations' intense close-quarters combat will mean that soldiers need more ammunition, more water, and meals denser in calories. More combat casualties and nonbattle injuries will result in greater demand for Class VIII materials. Other classes of supply will have similarly extraordinary requirements. The SCL could include LOG-PACs tailored for squads or other small elements. A difficulty is that the current depot system is unlikely to be flexible enough to handle such detailed needs with adequate responsiveness. It is therefore worth considering outsourcing or otherwise facilitating the preparation of these specialized support packages.[7]

ADAPTATION AND ANTICIPATION

> The IRA were getting better, because don't forget, they had their own intelligence—but the British army was getting better quicker.
>
> Charles Allen, *The Savage Wars of Peace,*
> writing of operations in Northern Ireland during the 1970s

The following subsections consider selected aspects of urban sustainment and movement and how anticipation and adaptation can enhance their effectiveness.

Fueling

Urban operations can complicate fuel distribution considerably. They demand constant adaptation as the nature of the urban terrain, mission, threat, and intensity of operations change over time and space. CSS leaders will have to find locations that provide ready access and egress for both fuel delivery and distribution, can be secured without too great a cost in manpower, and will not unneces-

---

[7]Insights on how to approach the problem might be gained from the U.S. Navy. The Naval Facilities Engineering Service Center is currently developing "Expeditionary Packaging Technology" that involves packing consumable supplies into ready-to-use modules subsequently shipped from the manufacturer to end user in unit loads without interim reconfiguration. The Navy goal is timely delivery of the correct quantities to the correct customer.

sarily endanger other facilities or personnel during either normal operations or in the case of fire. Ideally, any damage done to the local environment due to spills or traffic will be minimal. (It should be noted that these desirable properties apply equally to support and stability operations of which combat is not a component.) Finally, several small sites are preferred to one or two larger storage or distribution points so as to minimize the operational consequences should one such point be destroyed.

As in any deployment, bulk fuel delivery during urban operations will be provided via Defense Logistics Agency regional contracts and, to the extent needed to augment contract sources, that organization's wartime reserve stocks. Aircraft (bladder bird C-130s or KC-10s) may have to deliver initial stocks when regional fuel support cannot be established early enough to support requirements.[8] Innovative CSS leaders might be able to complement these traditional methods with several ad hoc initiatives given that urban areas are often locations in which large quantities of fuel are stored. Ports, airfields, and commercial petroleum-handling facilities can be designated as early targets for seizure, either to allow friendly forces to use the fuel on hand (after testing for suitability) or for storage of imported petroleum, oil, and lubricant (POL) products. Favorably sited filling stations might be similarly employed. The fact that stations often have adjacent garages makes them even more attractive; fueling units can maintain their vehicles or provide a site for mechanics to service and repair customer transport.

The vulnerability of fuel transporters and the difficulty of pulling combat vehicles far enough back from the line of contact to reach those trucks means that innovations are likely to be called for to augment doctrinal means of replenishment. Several techniques and emerging technological capabilities have application in this regard.

Urban CSS fuel sustainment operations might be well served by the use of available subterranean facilities. Sewers, underground parking structures, and basements are among the urban structures that offer prospective cover and concealment, minimizing CSS signatures and potentially reducing force protection manpower requirements.

---

[8]FM 3-20.96 (2d Coord Draft), Chapter 8.

Storing fuel in one location and running hoses from that point through sewer systems, buildings, or other concealed routes to supply interior or exterior storage or fueling points would further enhance security. This would minimize the impact of attacks on the "satellite" distribution locations, those most likely to be detected due to the level of activity around them and the number of vehicles in their vicinity. Were one fuel storage location to go dry, another at a different location could be employed with no change in fuel distribution points (given sufficient pumps and hose length). Alternative and secondary storage points would assume primary status while the empty one was resupplied (perhaps by a similar underground hose system). The concept is not without risk. Subterranean fuel leakage will present a danger of explosion without proper venting, the use of spark-suppressing gases, or other safety procedures.[9] It may be necessary to seal off or otherwise secure portions of underground systems to prevent interdiction or sabotage. Rebar, steel beams, and concrete anchors are among the materials that could be employed to block access points such as doorways, manholes, or the sewerage itself.

The current allocations of pump and hose assets for U.S. units might be insufficient should the organizations' fuel storage and distribution nodes be scattered in so dispersed a manner.[10] It is also possible that attempts to pump fluids from underground may exceed pump ca-

---

[9]Note that development of "binary fuels" akin to binary munitions would significantly reduce the danger of accidental detonations. Such development could involve putting an additive in fuels to make them less combustible during transit, a neutralizing agent being added during or before the fuel is pumped into vehicles or other equipment. To the authors' knowledge, no such capability is under development at this time.

[10]For example, the SBCT has a brigade support battalion (BSB) with the capability to store 56,000 gallons of fuel in its 14 Heavy Expanded Mobility Tactical Truck (HEMTT) tankers (each having a carrying capacity of 2,500 gallons) and 42 collapsible fuel pods (each capable of storing 500 gallons). With all of its vehicles fueled to maximum capacity, the SBCT's on-hand fuel exceeds 100,000 gallons. For fuel distribution, the unit has only 6 centrifugal pumps capable of pumping up to 125 gallons of fuel per minute. The brigade has 8 sets (25 feet each) of collapsible hose line for a total of a mere 200 feet. Planning assumptions for fueling are based upon resupply every other day.

At the time of this writing, SBCT echelon above brigade support is still being debated and analyzed. One consideration is to augment the SBCT with ten 5,000-gallon bulk tanker trucks that would be used to transport fuel from host nation support distribution points or the nearest sea point of debarkation (SPOD).

pacities. Experimentation is necessary to determine suitable pump capabilities, numbers of pumps, length of hose line, and storage capacity needed to support each unit type. Increases in hose length requirements present an obvious argument for developing lighter and less bulky hoses.

One U.S. Army system that is an obvious candidate for such testing is the currently available Assault Hoseline System (AHS), a bulk fuel distribution capability able to traverse a wide variety of terrain types. AHS consists of 14,000 feet of 4-inch collapsible hose and a pressure regulated pumping assembly that relies on a 350-GPM (gallons per minute) diesel pump. It can be suspended over gaps of up to two hundred feet.[11] A second contestant is the army's Rapidly Installed Fuel Transfer System (RIFTS), a heavy truck-transported bulk fuel distribution system under development at the time of publication. It includes pump, conduit, and other components capable of a minimum daily throughput of 850,000 gallons of fuel. Expected rates for laying conduit are between twenty and thirty miles daily; the system can handle a total length of conduit up to fifty miles.[12] Both of these systems depend on a soft-skinned vehicle for laying hose or conduit.

The Advanced Aviation Forward Area Refueling System (AAFARS, see Figure 2) might also address some of these needs. The AAFARS is a lightweight, modular, air- or ground-emplaced system initially designed to refuel aircraft at sites not accessible by ground transport or when the urgency of the situation requires rapid establishment or movement of forward refueling sites. It can simultaneously sustain four fueling points, each providing up to 55 GPM, or a single point capable of pumping at 90 GPM. AAFARS has 100 feet of collapsible hose line. Fuel is stored in 500-gallon pods (bladders). It takes four soldiers but 20 minutes to bring a site into operation. Sufficient numbers of AAFARS might provide the assets necessary to flexibly shift flows from one subterranean fuel pod to another as described above.

---

[11]Assault Hoseline System (AHS), PM Petroleum and Water Systems (PAWS), *http://peocscss.tacom.army.mil/pmFP/pm_paws/systems/ahs.htm.* Accessed October 18, 2002.

[12]Rapidly Installed Fuel Transfer System (RIFTS), PM Petroleum and Water Systems (PAWS), *http://peocscss.tacom.army.mil/pmFP/pm_paws/systems/rifts.htm.* Accessed October 18, 2002.

Figure 2—Advanced Aviation Forward Area Refueling System (AAFARS)

Urban contingencies could require point delivery of fuel, necessitating the transport of fuel directly to combat and other vehicles. The Naval Facilities Engineering Service Center "D-Day Mobile Fuel Distribution System" prototype (400 DMFD) represents a capability that could be delivered by helicopter, High-Mobility Multipurpose Wheeled Vehicle (HMMWV), or, alternatively, an armored logistics vehicle should one be fielded. The 400 DMFD is currently stored belowdecks on amphibious ships, where it is staged, fueled, and loaded onto an LCAC landing craft. It consists of a series of knock-down tanks that can be handled individually or in multiples.[13] Another option is the service's Load Handling System Modular Fuel Farm (LMFF). Each system includes ten 2,500-gallon tank racks and one pump rack, either of which can be deployed using Heavy Expanded Mobility Tactical Truck (HEMTT) vehicles. This full-spectrum system provides a rapidly emplaced fuel distribution system that can receive, store, and distribute fuel at a fraction of the

---

[13]"D-Day Mobile Fuel Distribution System," briefing provided by Buck Thomas, Naval Facilities Engineering Center, Point Hueneme, California. Received via email to Steven L. Hartman, September 25, 2002.

time required for a collapsible system.[14] This system is an excellent example of the potential benefits that could be attained were the services to coordinate and communicate CSS requirements, initiatives, procurement programs, and fielding schemes more diligently.

Water

That urban warfare is characterized by small maneuver elements with unusual task organizations considerably complicates CSS operations. The challenges are magnified in that these exceptional requirements extend to the individual soldier level. Other environments have particularly notable demands; increases in individuals' water needs in desert climes and increased caloric intake in cold-weather areas are two examples. But few environments have as many extraordinary demands at the individual soldier level as the urban setting. Like the desert fighter, the urban warrior needs more water. Like his cold-climate counterpart, he needs more calories. Men fighting in urban areas will also consume boots, weapons, ammunition, gloves, other uniform items, first aid supplies, and much else more quickly than anyone anywhere else. Each of these unusually high demand levels requires more of the CSS system and those who run it.

Considering sustainment concepts in this environment requires flexibility, initiative, and creativity. As is the case with ammunition and casualty statistics, a lack of quality data on urban consumption factors means that it will be difficult to gauge the appropriate balance between best guesses and quantities that overburden lift and indigenous capabilities. During early operations in Somalia, U.S. CSS leaders tracked the total numbers of personnel, vehicles, planes, and ships that arrived. Subsequent calculations of expected fuel and water demands made it evident that they would never be able to provide sufficient water at the standard rate of seven gallons daily per man. They eventually determined that reducing that rate to three gallons was appropriate based on the assumption that initially no one would be doing laundry and that there was no need to plan for

---

[14]Load Handling System-Modular Fuel Farm (LMFF), PM Petroleum and Water Systems   (PAWS),   *http://www.peocscss.tacom.army.mil/pmFP/pm_paws/systems/ lmff.htm*, accessed October 18, 2002.

medical water usage until the field hospital arrived. A similar process allowed them to better estimate actual fuel usage requirements.[15]

Several technologies that could help to address urban operations' increased water demands exist or are under development. The Canteen Insert Water Purifier (CIWP) is a system capable of sustaining a soldier for up to two weeks, eliminating much of the need for water purification and transport.[16] The CIWP provides filtration by disinfecting water as it is drawn through the straw by the user. The straw is compatible for use with the one- and two-quart Army canteens or from any freestanding water source. No tablets are needed; the disinfectant is on-demand. The CIWP treats 6 liters of water per day for up to 14 days from any fresh water source (providing a total of 84 liters of potable water). Current fielding plans would allocate the system on the basis of one per squad. Farther into the future, research is under way to create potable water from engine exhaust. The objective is to generate 1.4 pounds of water for every pound of fuel burned, the product subsequently being filtered to drinkable standards.[17] This capability is unfortunately not envisioned to be ready prior to the period of Objective Force fielding.

Pending development or fielding of such capabilities, a means of supply superior to bottled water is necessary. Storage and distribution could be executed in a manner virtually identical to that for fuel as described above. Testing to determine pump, bladder, and hose requirements would be necessary, just as it is for fuel. Options for bulk water purification to feed such a storage and distribution sys-

---

[15]COL Stephen P. Hayward, *Personal Experience Monograph, DISCOM S-3, Somalia (29 Dec 92–25 Feb 93)*, Carlisle Barracks, PA: U.S. Army War College, 1998, p. 4.

[16]"Canteen Insert Water Purifier," TARDEC Water and Wastewater web site, *http://www.tacom.army.mil/tardec/division/peth2o/peth2o.htm*, accessed January 26, 2000.

[17]William Purdue interview conducted by Steven Hartman, Fort Lee, VA, April 17, 2002; and briefing slides provided by The Quartermaster School Petroleum and Water Department, Fort Lee, VA, April 17, 2002.

Obtaining 1.4 pounds of water from a single pound of fuel might at first appear to be a violation of the conservation of mass principle. However, fuel combustion is not a closed system. The two main chemical byproducts of burning fuel are carbon dioxide and water, each of which is created by adding oxygen atoms to carbon-hydrogen chains in the process of burning or "oxidation." The extra oxygen atoms from the air make the water and account for the product being heavier than the original fuel. The authors thank Matthew Lewis for providing this clarification.

RAND *MR1717-3a*

Figure 3—Lightweight Water Purifier

tem include setting up 3,000 gallon per hour (GPH) Reverse Osmosis Water Purification Units (ROWPU). The 1,500-GPH Tactical Water Purification System (TWPS) and Light Water Purifiers (LWP, see Figure 3) are among the systems that could complement or be used in lieu of ROWPU for smaller units.[18] The LWP is an HMMWV-mounted system capable of producing 125 GPH of potable water from a fresh water source and 75 GPH from salt water.[19] For distribution, there is the Tactical Water Distribution System (TWDS) that includes pumps, two 20,000-gallon fabric collapsible tanks, and 10-mile hose line segments that could distribute potable water over a considerable urban operational area.[20] The Load Handling System Water Tank Rack ("Hippo") system provides army units with 2,000 gallons of storage capacity per tank, a size feasible for delivery and

[18]"Tactical Water Purification System," *http://peocscss.tacom.army.mil/pmFP/ pm_paws/systems/twps1500.htm*, accessed October 21, 2002.

[19]"Lightweight Water Purifier," *http://peocscss.tacom.army.mil/pmFP/pm_paws/ systems/lwp.htm*, accessed October 21, 2002.

[20]"Tactical Water Purification Systems (TWPS)," *http://peocscss.tacom.army.mil/pmFP/ pm_paws/systems/twds.htm*, accessed October 21, 2002.

storage in warehouses, parking garages, or other suitable structures. The hard shell tanks can be transported and up- or downloaded using a HEMTT Load Handling System (LHS).[21] For sea-based (or sea-supported) operations, the water source could be a ship-based bulk water purification system.

Power

Power requirements will be notably troublesome during contingencies in built-up areas.[22] Contracting from local power suppliers is desirable, but operational requirements demand that backup constantly be on hand. A soldier operating in Haiti recalled that "if you didn't have a surge protector and [uninterruptible power supply] connected to your computer, you couldn't function because the Haitian power fluctuated and frequently went out completely during the day. Backup generator power would come on in 5–10 minutes, [often] not soon enough . . . I guess the lesson here is never to be totally dependent on local resources, especially key things like HQs and hospitals." He additionally noted that complete reliance on local power suppliers makes the friendly force vulnerable to coercion should the provider threaten to or actually suspend provision.[23] The same is true of any locally provided resource, whether power, water, vehicle transportation, or other supplies and services. CSS leaders and commanders need to balance the inherent risks in local contracting with the benefits gained. Plans should be in place to either replace local services/supplies if they are suspended or tailor operations to account for reduced amounts of indigenously supplied resources.

In keeping with the constant need to consider second- and higher-order effects during urban contingencies, the same soldier further noted that the power-related consequences of the U.S. Army's increasing reliance on digitization will also affect Class III require-

---

[21]Load Handling System Water Tank Rack "Hippo," PM Petroleum and Water (PAWS), *http://peocscss.tacom.army.mil/pmFP/pm_paws/systems/hippo.htm*, accessed October 18, 2002.

[22]Comment by Major Kevin Born, CASCOM, based on his experiences during deployment to Haiti.

[23]Kevin Born, email to Steven Hartman, "Fuel in UO, Part II," April 16, 2002.

ments. He noted that "one of the things that I think has been over-looked is the large power consumption requirement of a digitized force. Right now in the SBCT and Force XI Division, all of the Force XXI Battle Command, Brigade and Below (FBCB2) computer systems are mounted on vehicles. So what happens when you have vehicle mounted systems like this? Even if the vehicle is stationary the operator is going to have to run the engine periodically through the day to maintain the charge on the batteries."[24]

Air Resupply

There will be instances when the tactical situation will not allow ground resupply. Leaders will look to helicopters or unmanned aerial vehicles (UAVs) to fill the void, at least for cases involving the delivery of the limited amounts of material feasible using such means. As hovering aircraft have proved very vulnerable to urban fires, an alternative means of delivery is necessary. The "speed ball" concept involves rotary-wing delivery of preconfigured loads prepackaged in aviation kit bags, duffel bags, or other containers to protect supplies against impact. The containers are encased in bubble wrap; the helicopter flies as close to the receiving unit or designated drop point as possible, momentarily reduces speed to execute the drop, and then leaves immediately (see Figure 4). In urban areas, rooftops or secured drop zones such as small parking lots or playing fields are prospective delivery points.[25]   Many supplies likely to require speedball delivery will be difficult to package (e.g., plasma, water). It is therefore advisable that the transportation communities conduct peacetime experimentation with the objective of providing guidance on packaging techniques, speed and angle of drop, and other pertinent factors.

While this method of aerial delivery may be viable for delivery of small quantities of supplies, ways of providing ground forces with larger quantities will be essential to minimize the number of aircraft exposed to enemy fire. The U.S. Army continues work on the Precision, Extended Glide, and Air Drop System (PEGASYS) capable of de-

---

[24]Ibid.

[25]FM 3-06.11, p. 13-12.

Figure 4—"Speed Ball" Supply Delivery

livering material via unmanned aircraft.[26] PEGASYS consists of a
family of aerodynamic airfoils; these systems vary in offset capabilities (glide ratios) and payload weights. The latter range from small,
light bundles to deliveries weighing up to 2,200 pounds (with concepts for future systems having capacities up to 42,000 pounds).[27]

---

[26]"US Army Precision, Extended Glide Airdrop System (PEGASYS)," Briefing by Ed
Doucette, U.S. Army Natick Soldier Center, May 2, 2003; and "Precision Airdrop
Distribution Concept of Support for Future Military Operations (Draft)," draft paper,
Airdrop/Aerial Delivery Directorate, U.S. Army Natick Soldier Center, undated.

[27]Mr. Edward Doucette, Airdrop/Aerial Delivery Directorate, U.S. Army Natick Soldier
Center, telephone interview with Steve Hartman, May 14, 2002.

RAND *MR1717-5*

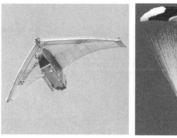 

Figure 5—Unmanned Aerial Supply Delivery Systems

PEGASYS incorporates an Airborne Guidance Unit (AGU) that employs GPS technology and other sensors. The system has proved accurate during testing, providing the ability to deliver rigged loads to a touchdown point with a circular error probable (CEP) of 25 to 100 meters.[28] Based on winds, payload, and glide ratio, standoff distances for nonpowered flight can range up to fifty kilometers; significantly greater distances can be achieved using powered versions. It is conceivable that delivery could be made to parking structures, parks, playing fields, or even the rooftops of buildings. System feasibility for use in urban areas merits testing, as wind conditions amid buildings can be very unpredictable. It is likely that problems involving such eccentric urban wind patterns, tall structures' impact on angles of approach and landing, intermittent loss of GPS signals, and risks involving collateral damage and noncombatant injury are among issues that need addressing. (See Figure 5. The picture on the right shows a light payload of approximately 1,500 pounds. That on the left is an experimental Semi-Rigid Wing Test Flight with a 500-pound load.)[29]

---

[28]CEPs of this size may not suffice for urban operations. Errors of this range could put drops on the other side of buildings or even in another block. A television-guided system might supply the additional accuracy necessary by replicating a manned drop capable of terminal adjustments. Other possible components of a solution include assumption of terminal guidance by those receiving the supplies or a net recovery system strung between buildings on the drop zone.

[29]Images are from the American Institute of Aeronautics and Astronomy Aerodynamic Decelerator System Technical Committee, *http://www.engr.uconn.edu,* accessed May 14, 2002.

Sea-Based Resupply

Another interesting approach to urban force sustainment involves supply from the sea. Sea-based CSS offers enhanced security by reducing logistics footprints ashore. Because the U.S. Army is a force projection service, securing airfields and ports will often be a prerequisite to follow-on operations in a country's interior. These airfields and ports are frequently adjacent to bodies of water accessible to U.S. Navy vessels. Being able to capitalize on naval lift, standoff, firepower, and support infrastructure during such undertakings will therefore offer commanders valuable alternatives to more remote land basing. Potential systems include the heavy lift capabilities of Large Medium-Speed Roll-on/Roll-off ships (LMSR). One LMSR can carry an entire U.S. Army task force of 58 tanks, 48 other tracked vehicles, and over 900 wheeled vehicles.

Each vessel has a carrying capacity of more than 380,000 square feet. In addition, LMSRs have a sluing stern ramp and a removable ramp that services two side ports to ease vehicle access or egress from the vessel. Interior ramps between decks simplify traffic flow once cargo is loaded. A pair of 110-ton single pedestal twin cranes make it possible to load and unload cargo where shore-side infrastructure is limited or nonexistent. There are plans for adding 19 LMSRs to the Navy's inventory, giving the military an additional five million square feet of projection capacity.[30]

There are two options if a contingency requires intra-theater movement or transporting materiel to shore from deep-draft vessels. The army's Theater Support Vessel (TSV) is still under development. It will have a payload-carrying area of 30,000 square feet and a 1,250-STON haul capacity. Its range will be up to 4,700 nautical miles with survivability in conditions in excess of Sea State 7. The vessel will be fully communications interoperable, thus allowing enroute mission planning.

A second intra-theater vessel is the Landing Craft Air Cushion (LCAC). (See Figure 6.) LCAC are currently employed to transport

---

[30]United States Navy Fact File, "Large, Medium-speed, roll-on/roll-off ships—T-AKR," United States Navy Fact File, *http://www.chinfo.navy.mil/navpalib/factfile/ ships/ship-takr2.html,* accessed June 14, 2002.

USMC Marine Air/Ground Task Force (MAGTF) assault element weapon systems, equipment, cargo, and personnel from ship to shore and across the beach. The vessel is capable of carrying a payload of from 60 to 75 tons (to include the largest combat vehicles) and operating from existing and planned well-deck ships. Unlike Surface Effect Ships (SES), no portion of the LCAC hull penetrates the water; the ship rides approximately four feet above the surface, able to pass over minor obstacles. Equipment such as trucks and tracked vehicles can disembark via ramps located both forward and aft. The ship is capable of launching amphibious assaults from points over the horizon, thereby decreasing risk to ships and personnel. Due to the vessel's over-the-beach capability, the LCAC has utility for operations along more than 80 percent of the world's coastlines.[31]

RAND *MR1717-6*

Figure 6—Landing Craft Air Cushion (LCAC)

---

[31]"Landing Craft, Air Cushion," Military Analysis Network, *http://www.fas.org/man/dod-101/sys/ship/lcac.htm*, accessed June 14, 2002.

The Naval Facilities Service Center is developing a Sea-Cache Submersible Fuel System that would provide 100,000 gallons of near-shore or deep-water underwater fuel storage, a capability that could reduce LCAC or other amphibious shipping turnaround times. An LCAC, for example, would only have to travel approximately a nautical mile from shore to be safely refueled from the undersea bladders. This system could mitigate needs for constructing and securing large land-based fuel storage facilities were a capability developed to pump fuel from the submerged bladders to shore.

Ground-Based Resupply

As fighting in 1993 Mogadishu reminded us, it is often risky to send a convoy of soft-skinned vehicles into streets swept by fire, exposing the occupants to snipers, booby-traps, and anti-tank weapons. Using armored vehicles for LOGPAC push offers increased survivability and force protection. One option would be the use of Abrams tanks in a sort of Red Ball Express to bring critical support to an engaged fighting force. Creating and prepositioning urban forward logistics elements (FLEs) to support critical points identified during CSS IPB analysis gives sustainers an additional means of enhancing operational responsiveness. These FLEs could be stationary ISP locations that provide an opportunity to replenish, rest, or repair. Alternatively, urban CSS leaders should consider developing mobile FLEs that move from their predesignated locations to dash in and provide needed services such as resupply, recovery, or casualty evacuation.

Were sustainment based on resupply from a stationary FLE, a dismounted infantry leader would have to consider how to move supplies back to his fighting position with the minimum loss of fighting power. The SKEDCO litter (fielded with U.S. Army forces since the mid-1980s) is an innovative means of evacuating wounded or moving supplies within an urban area. Given the right terrain conditions, this lightweight system allows one man to evacuate a wounded soldier or bring supplies forward. It is also easily prepared for helicopter extraction.[32]

---

[32]Geocities, "SKED: How to Evacuate Your Wounded Soldiers . . ." *http://www. geocities.com/equipmentshop/skedinstructions.htm*, accessed July 1, 2002.

A human remains body bag or stretcher can also provide a way to move supplies. The bags are waterproof and can be hauled by two soldiers if not overloaded. Loads can be pulled across roads or other open areas using ropes thrown or launched from one side of the gap to the other (perhaps using a system similar to that for recovering wounded soldiers). It is important to clearly stencil the containers with the word "SUPPLIES" using bright colors to designate which bags contain supplies.[33]

Finally, there are reports of an innovative Russian means of delivering small quantities of supplies to isolated forces. An arms firm has developed a small recoilless launch system that weighs thirty pounds. It is claimed that it can be shoulder-fired to launch containers with food, medicine, water, or other materials up to three kilometers.[34]

The size of mouse holes, windows, or even some doorways can make it difficult if not impossible for soldiers to pass through these openings while wearing a full combat load. Special Forces soldiers operating in Afghanistan during 2002 found that they sometimes needed to shed their gear to pass through doors much narrower and shorter than is the norm in the United States.[35] Heavy loads can also prove impractical during urban assaults. Lessons learned during actions in 1989 Panama included a recommendation to "issue an assault pack similar to the old butt pack for carrying basic load ammunition and other items. The rucksack was too large for the final assault and for MOUT operations."[36]

Feeding soldiers at the cutting edge during urban operations is doubly difficult. Not only does the transport of meals involve considerable risk, but the number of calories available in MREs and other

---

[33]FM 3-06.11, p. 13-13.

[34]Nikolai Gorshkov, "Russia's 'Humanitarian Weapon,'" British Broadcasting System, 15:34 GMT, July 30, 2002. The authors thank Dr. Theodore Karasik for bringing this source to their attention.

[35]Russell W. Glenn, Special Forces interview, McDill Air Force Base, September 19, 2002.

[36]*Operation Just Cause Lessons Learned: Volume III-Intelligence, Logistics, & Equipment,* Fort Leavenworth, KS: U.S. Army Center for Lessons Learned, October 1990, no page numbers.

existent meal packets may also fall short of soldier needs. Russian leaders in Grozny, for example, thought a soldier required 5,000 calories daily, considerably above the 3,800 calories provided on average to a U.S. soldier consuming three MREs. (Though it appears in literature on the conflict, it is unknown where the Russian value of 5,000 calories originally came from.) The matter is not one of simply having fighters eat more; a warrior's stomach can hold only so much. Testing is needed to determine daily caloric demands during urban contingencies, but evidence implies that meals designed to provide more sustenance per unit of food weight are called for.

Scientists at the Department of Defense's Combat Feeding Program have begun conceptual research on an innovative means of addressing this requirement. Their Transdermal Nutrient Delivery System (TNDS) provides soldiers with what looks much like the nicotine patches that smokers use to help them quit. The TNDS patch is attached to the skin and thereafter transfers nutrients into the soldier's system via a "microdialysis" process. This patch would provide warfighters with the means to maintain acceptable performance for a day or two until a meal can be consumed.[37]

Scientists are also investigating several other food-related means of enhancing soldier performance. One involves a tiny microchip processor imbedded in the skin that would determine a soldier's metabolic needs and then transfer the needed nutrients via a micro-electrical mechanical system (MEMS) that opens the pores of the skin and transfers nutrients directly into the capillaries.

COMMAND AND CONTROL

> The key to their success, as with the rest of the battalion, was the opportunity to conduct rehearsals on or near the same terrain on which they fought.
>
> Clarence E. Briggs
> *Operation Just Cause*, 1989

---

[37]Jerry Darsch, Department of Defense Combat Feeding Program, Natick Soldiers Systems Center, telephone interview with Steven L. Hartman, October 4, 2002. Microdialysis research continues at Clemson University.

The larger numbers of nodes requiring CSS support combine with delays in turnaround times due to navigation difficulties, wear and tear on vehicles, and myriad other factors to make effective management of transport assets and supplies absolutely vital during urban operations. Leaders will find that strict discipline, innovation, and maintenance of flexibility in plans and operations will all play a role in this regard. Maneuver units must not hoard haul capability.[38] Food planning has to account for the unauthorized issuance of MREs and other food to members of a disadvantaged population. Soldiers will give up their own rations to relieve the suffering of those around them even when explicitly ordered not to do so.

City streets offer a palette of challenges that demand astute preparation of soldiers in specialties from vehicle driver to combat engineer. NATO doctrine warns that "pre-deployment training should include unique requirements for drivers, crowd control and gathering information from and negotiating with civilians." U.S. Army guidance further advises that "drivers must be well trained, rehearsed, and alert to recognize and avoid potential mines and minefields (such as driving in the same tracks as the vehicle in front) and to react rapidly to ambushes."[39] Planners who fail to compensate for longer transport times in built-up areas due to traffic density, lower speeds, narrow streets, difficulty of navigation, and other factors will find themselves chronically unable to meet their own timetables. Getting it right the first time is only the initial step. Change during urban operations is inevitable. Planners need to designate alternate routes, specify secondary means of accomplishing sustainment tasks, and maintain the flexibility in operations to deal with such dramatic changes as the introduction of chemical weapons or eruption of public demonstrations.[40] Leaders need to vary routes used so that adversaries do not determine patterns and ambush friendly force soldiers and marines (or so that noncombatants do not use such information to similarly "ambush" convoys in order to steal their con-

---

[38]"Trucks and helicopters are critical transportation assets. Units must release these assets following mission completion." *Operation Just Cause Lessons Learned*, no page numbers.

[39]"Improving Land Armaments: Lessons from the Balkans," RTO-TR-AC/323(SAS-041)TP/, Brussels, Belgium: North Atlantic Treaty Organization, November 2001, p. 5.3.1; and FM 3-06, p. 9-16.

[40]FM 3-20.96, p. 8-49.

tents). In Haiti, U.S. forces built a route around heavily congested areas, as "it was the only way to avoid the immense traffic congestion inherent to the city center during the day. The only way you could get around [within the city of Port-au-Prince] with any freedom was to travel between 2400 hrs and 0500 hrs."[41]

Tactical movement planners who do not coordinate with their CSS counterparts will find both combat and sustainment operations threatened with failure.[42] Routes for attack, withdrawal, movement of reserves, replenishment, casualty evacuation, use by civilian refugees, and EPW egress to the rear all need to be incorporated into a plan, as do alternate and secondary routes for each. Despite the plethora of traveled ways in most towns and cities, the times when there are enough routes to be able to assign each function to its own street will be rare. Movement timetables, strict discipline in enforcing those schedules, and prioritization of route usage all need to be part of urban movement plans. Engineer units need to be assigned mobility responsibilities and locations at which they can preposition supporting equipment.[43]

EXTRAORDINARY DEMANDS

Points of debarkation remote from enemy forces and unopposed arrivals in a theater provide U.S. forces time to "shake out" combat units before meeting the foe. Ports and airfields in contested urban areas raise the possibility of units having to roll off the ramp and directly into combat. Restrictions on vehicles loaded for transport make such scenarios especially worrisome. USAF or weight restrictions, for example, can mean that combat vehicles' fuel tanks contain very little and that the systems include but a few rounds of ammunition during air transit. Other critical vehicle components (e.g., bolt-on armor and tow bars) might arrive on separate lifts, especially if the movement is via C-130 aircraft.[44] CSS planners will have to work

---

[41]Major Kevin Born's comments on Lawrence E. Casper, *Falcon Brigade: Combat and Command in Somalia and Haiti,* Boulder, CO: Lynne Rienner, 2001.

[42]FM 3-20.96, p. 8-50.

[43]Ibid.

[44]Larry M. DeRoche, interview with Russell W. Glenn, Fort Lewis, WA, November 28, 2002.

closely with their maneuver counterparts to assess risks and define the limits of the possible. They can also favorably influence the tactical situation via well-considered pre-landing preparations. The expected availability of immediate sources of fuel (either contracted from local sources or purchased from indigenous fuel supplies such as gas stations) will potentially leave more airlifts available for early delivery of ammunition or selected other mission-critical items.

Disembarking vehicles not yet ready to fight is only one source of difficulty for arriving units. The need to augment those systems will further burden CSS distribution systems. Operation Just Cause Lessons Learned, for example, recommend the carrying of at least one five-gallon can on every vehicle to ensure that crews have sufficient water. The cans also mean that minimum time is spent replenishing, as empties are quickly exchanged for full vessels.[45] Another lesson noted that urban actions consume great quantities of chemlites, which are used to mark cleared buildings, friendly positions, and breaching and link-up points. Infrared chemlites were particularly in demand, as too many visible sources of light compromised friendly unit locations and created confusion on the battlefield.[46]

Other exceptional requirements relate to needs at the individual rifleman level. For example, infantrymen often desire the issue of M4 carbines in lieu of M16 rifles when fighting in cities. The shorter-barreled weapons are easier to move and maneuver within tight spaces. The fraction of a second less that it takes to bring the smaller weapon to bear on a target can be the difference between survival and death during the less-than-25-meter engagements that are typical of street fighting. Means of breaking into rooms, through fences, or breaching other obstacles nonexplosively are needed when noncombatants are in the area or explosives use is impractical. Oversized wire cutters, axes, bolt cutters, crowbars, and similar instruments will be called for. Grappling hooks and small fire extinguishers similarly proved valuable during Operation Just Cause actions in 1989.[47]

---

[45]*Operation Just Cause Lessons Learned,* no page numbers.

[46]Ibid.

[47]Ibid.

It is a given that units carrying only Spartan support will have to maintain strict supply discipline until more robust means of sustaining them are in place. Such units may find that the time until replenishment takes place may be extended considerably if their mission is one in which support of the civilian population takes priority. The density of civilians in urban areas means that a force's CSS capabilities might be insufficient to support the simultaneous conduct of large-scale support and combat operations. Chances are good that the situation will worsen over time as refugees from the surrounding countryside flock toward locations where assistance is known to be available.

Quantity is only one measure of how difficult urban challenges can be. Another is variety in the character of those challenges. Depending on the social norms involved, the presence of large numbers of indigenous females or very young children in the supported population could respectively influence the mix of hygiene or food products brought into a theater. It might also influence leader decisions about the gender mix of medical, military police, and other unit types. Awareness of social norms *before* load planning could make the difference between a public relations coup and unnecessary embarrassment. Distribution of proscribed foods, failure to plan for separate shelters or hygiene facilities for males and females, or expectations that male doctors will be allowed to provide care to indigenous women are among the more obvious issues that could slow the building of goodwill and the alleviation of local suffering.

The proximity of the enemy and the need to sometimes stockpile supplies forward for purposes of operational responsiveness mean that the adversary will at times threaten capture of these stores. Units need to plan for the destruction of supplies and equipment (other than medical) that cannot be evacuated in such contingencies. This requirement presupposes having a means on hand for executing such rapid destruction.[48]

---

[48]FM 3-20.96, p. 8-50.

CONCLUDING REMARKS

Existing doctrine, training, and structures, together with careful consideration of the challenges of urban areas, will provide an appropriate basis for initial adaptations, command and control procedures, and general adjustments to the extraordinary demands inherent in urban missions as discussed above. Close monitoring of ongoing and future operation lessons learned and continuous adjustment of these initial estimates and approaches during the conduct of operations will further enhance readiness both during ongoing missions and in subsequent undertakings. This awareness of the need to constantly adapt is essential to all facets of CSS urban support, even those such as maintenance of a force's equipment that might at first glance seem to be little affected by built-up areas.

Chapter Six

FIXING

Good logistics is combat power.

William G. Pagonis
Moving Mountains, 1992

"Fixing" responsibilities take on a new look when a force operates in a built-up area. All the traditional tasks remain, among them vehicle repair and recovery, maintenance of communications capabilities, calibration, and weapons care. Oversight of the infrastructure on which noncombatants rely for daily needs can fall to CSS units or contractors hired and supervised by them. It has been noted that uniforms and equipment items abused by harsh urban surfaces will increase the demand on maintenance providers as well as those responsible for obtaining replacements. Further, the type of wear and tear is likely to be more diverse than is encountered in other operating environments: the urban environment presents a denser and more heterogeneous concentration of hazards. Vehicles are threatened not only by direct fire from their front, rear, or sides and by mines underneath; engagement from upper stories and rooftops will be commonplace. Impact by falling debris or collisions with walls, overhangs, and curbs will cause both incidental and mission-critical damage. More frequent jarring against such surfaces translates to more frequent calibration of equipment. Routine scheduled vehicle care will be vital in addition to aggressive PLL management and responsive emergency maintenance procedures. Performing scheduled maintenance on HMMWV tires, for example, proved vital to maintaining their run-flat capabilities during 1989 combat operations in Panama City.[1]

The above argue for deploying a robust maintenance capacity with any unit contemplating urban action. The SBCT's slim organic fixing capability has raised concerns in this regard. Stryker Brigade Combat Teams each have a forward maintenance company (FMC) that is responsible for both organizational and direct support maintenance. The FMC has four combat repair teams (CRT), one to support each of the brigade's three maneuver battalions and the fourth to provide such service to the reconnaissance, surveillance, and target acquisition (RSTA) squadron. Unfortunately, the FMC's organic capacity to support these elements is very limited. Higher headquarters can augment the FMC with a maintenance platoon from a Combat Service Support Company (CSSC). This platoon provides automotive, armament, and electronics support not available in the FMC. This augmentation may not be available until well after the initial arrival of the FMC and much of the remainder of the SBCT, however. It is in this regard that the SBCT's fixing capabilities raise concerns. Without CSSC augmentation, many working with the brigade doubt that the organization can appropriately maintain its organic systems. Obviously such doubts are of even greater concern given the high tempo of operations likely in urban areas. A modification of current structures that helps to address these concerns is currently under consideration. The change would assign a CSSC to each SBCT as an organic asset. Based on input from the field given to the authors of this study, such a revision is highly desirable.

Several maintenance enhancements beyond this organizational augmentation are currently under consideration. These include (1) purchase of Stryker Operational Readiness Floats (ORF), (2) improvements in Ready-to-Fight (RTF) stocks, and (3) augmentation of current prescriptions for Stryker authorized stockage levels (ASL). Research is in progress to determine which single option or combination of these alternatives would best improve SBCT readiness at acceptable cost.

---

[1] Operation Just Cause Lessons Learned, no page numbers.

The SBCT is not alone. Other units may similarly need to bolster maintenance assets or allocate them in nontraditional ways. The tendency toward greater dispersion of armored vehicles during urban contingencies, for example (e.g., assigning one tank per squad or platoon of dismounted infantry), will strain the vehicles' parent unit capacity to sustain and maintain the systems and cause an overburdening of fixing capabilities akin to those that raise concerns about SBCT deployments.

These extraordinary support demands require decisive CSS command and control and skillful management maintenance resources. Non-mission-capable items have to be quickly identified and, if appropriate, stripped of usable parts before rapidly being evacuated from the area of operations.[2] Timely situational awareness about a unit's equipment readiness posture, repair parts status, and maintenance support capabilities is essential to making the correct decisions that will allow it to maintain a robust operational tempo during urban operations.

ADAPTATION AND ANTICIPATION

Fixing forces will often deploy well forward in order to accomplish their missions. Given the difficulty of navigating in built-up areas and the ease with which an enemy can infiltrate friendly positions, these sustainers will be uncharacteristically exposed to adversary fire, theft, or attacks by hungry or hateful members of the indigenous population. Responsiveness in providing battle damage assessment and repair (BDAR) and other fixing support means that CSS personnel will operate on contested terrain more frequently than usual. Nowhere is such responsiveness more important than when a disabled vehicle blocks others from passing on a street swept by enemy fire. Leaving the crippled vehicle in position means that those behind are "sitting ducks." Having a means of hooking and dragging the vehicle out of the way or positioning heavy vehicles in convoys so that they can push those that are blocking progress is advisable. Alternatively, commanders can require that maintenance or recovery assets be included in every vehicle movement. The objective is to

---

[2]Each CRT is equipped with two Heavy Expanded Mobility Tactical Truck (HEMTT) wreckers.

avoid leaving friendly systems on city streets. Temporarily abandoning a disabled vehicle may expose it to stripping by indigenous personnel even when enemy action is not a threat. (Leaving the vehicle crew with the inoperable system for security purposes could expose it to danger as well.) It is for these and similar reasons that U.S. Army doctrine recommends that CSS and maneuver leaders keep the repair and support teams well forward.[3] If a vehicle must be abandoned, operators should remove or destroy critical equipment. Maintenance units will similarly have to be aware of vital components that should not fall into enemy or noncombatant hands. Orders or standing operating procedures (SOPs) should designate which components are targets for such destruction. Good training will ensure that appropriate personnel practice removal and destruction procedures. Future provision of a remote means of destruction (e.g., a limited-area electromagnetic pulse for electronic or electro-magnetic components) would be highly desirable.

A "recover or lose" maintenance policy seems to provide an ironic contrast to that of "soldier treat thyself." Whereas earlier discussion suggested that wounded soldiers and their comrades might be better served by a policy of *not* exposing the uninjured via attempting costly rescue attempts, here the authors recommend rapid vehicle recovery. The contrast between the two policies is less stark than it at first seems. Vehicle recovery under fire is by no means proposed; it is to be undertaken as soon as possible after such immediate danger has passed so as to deny the indigenous population the opportunity to strip or otherwise further damage a system.

The high rates of vehicle attrition expected during urban operations, especially combat operations as demonstrated in 1973 Suez City and 1994–95 Grozny, means that rapidly repairing and returning systems to a fight will be crucial. Offshore repair might be a feasible option depending on the availability of land-based facilities suitable for repair and the ability of a force to secure these sites. Rotary-wing assets could lift lighter vehicles to the decks of waiting ships should the offshore option be employed. This would free limited onshore repair capabilities to focus on heavier systems for which such removal is impractical. Alternatively, given the fielding of LCAT or other over-

---

[3]FM 3-20.96, p. 8-49.

the-beach heavy-lift sea vessels, even a ground force's heaviest systems could be evacuated.

Contractors are increasingly relied on to maintain selected U.S. equipment. Many of these systems will never be maintained by military personnel throughout their life cycle. It is likely that contractors will also be responsible for providing repair parts for the equipment they are to repair. Some parts provided by such contractors are not type-classified with a military part number; they instead retain their original equipment manufacturers (OEM) part number. It is a given that Standard Army Maintenance System (SAMS) stock levels have to be checked to ensure they are sufficient for the higher urban operations attrition rates. CSS managers also need to monitor individual contractor plans for maintaining parts in suitable numbers. Given the expectation of high vehicle attrition during urban operations, it is advisable to consider requisitioning those items expected to be consumed at greater rates (e.g., tires) and establishing onshore higher-echelon maintenance facilities to which evacuated vehicles can be taken.

Although the near future might not allow for fundamental vehicle re-design in support of CSS activities, it is nevertheless worth embarking on a path toward developing vehicles and equipment that can be better tailored to suit the evolving needs of urban (and other types of) conflict. These could include steps taken to render units better able to conduct repairs and perform controlled substitutions. Modularity and appliqué/add-on components are potential approaches in this regard. Rapid replacement of easily identified and replaced modules makes it easier to quickly return a vehicle to operable status. More than merely a repair process, modularity can also expand functionality. A vehicle that can accept a variety of modules on a generic bed can carry a load of supplies on one tasking, later installing a repair module that makes it a field maintenance station were a mechanic driving or riding shotgun (much as the previously mentioned addition of a medical module would facilitate a vehicle's use as an ambulance).[4] If a disabled vehicle required evacuation, a winch module could be mounted and the vehicle immediately dis-

---

[4]"Shotgun" is a seat in a vehicle next to the driver, the implication being that the individual has the responsibility to provide security should the vehicle be threatened, just as did the persons who sat next to Old West stagecoach drivers.

patched. Such innovations will be especially valuable in urban contingencies where convoluted routes, communications difficulties, and high vehicle demand mean that response times for specific systems will at times be slow.

Other enhancements to urban operations maintenance and repair capabilities will come from technological evolution (e.g., more robust materials) or exploiting particular local opportunities (e.g., a local black market in spare parts). Near-term solutions will be the product of innovations and adaptations to doctrine, training, and administrative efficiency more than technological development.[5]

COMMAND AND CONTROL

It will be CSS planners who dictate what urban facilities are important to their plans. Some of these will always be important and should at a minimum be identified in the SOPs of units that will have the greatest opportunity to locate and report their whereabouts

---

[5]In the longer term, promising technological solutions could revolutionize maintenance and repair tasks. A sampling of such potential breakthroughs include:

Regenerative materials and composites: Significant advances have already been made in the development of "self-healing" materials, an example of which is a transparent organic polymeric material that can repeatedly mend itself after the infliction of mild damage. University of California, Los Angeles (UCLA) chemists and engineers conducting exotic materials research have produced a plastic called Automend that consists of interlocking molecular subunits, which together form a single giant macromolecule. If a product constructed with Automend cracks while in use, as might an electronic device that heats and cools frequently, it repairs itself during the first heating cycle following the damage. The restored area regains approximately 60 percent of its original strength.

"Smart" materials: For almost a decade, materials researchers have sought to embed controls that would allow for control of a material's properties to best meet the demands of the task at hand. Recent field tests have demonstrated that properties such as shape, conductivity, and vibration control can be "programmed" into a material. This would allow for generic replacement spares that replace more than one type of damaged component and thereby reducing the number of spare type in inventory.

Nano-manufactured or ultra-robust materials: Revolutionary materials constructed from sheets of "Buckytubes" (Buckminsterfullerence, or C^{60}) offer the possibility of vastly stronger components with much-reduced weights. Although development of such materials is longer term (in excess of five years) than the innovations previously mentioned, it nevertheless holds significant implications for vehicle and equipment durability, system recovery or transport, and spare parts.

during operations (e.g., reconnaissance, transportation, and military police units and aviation organizations). Others will be of significance only during specific types of missions or under given operational conditions. Those pertinent to fixing operations will be more or less valuable depending on whether indigenous resources will play a significant role in maintaining the force. CSS planners need to identify requirements during IPB analysis and bring them to the attention of any personnel whose tasks involve travels through the area of operations. Sites of potential value include automotive repair shops, foundries, junkyards, scrap-metal dealers, machine shops, and similar sources of material, facilities, or services. These sites will potentially serve as urban repair shops, alternate or supplemental sources for parts, distribution points, safe havens for evacuated damaged vehicles, or one or more of the many functions falling under the purview of CSS soldier responsibilities. As is the case with caches and any other facility, security must be a part of such analysis. Modifying SOPs and disseminating the changes will be especially valuable for units operating in urban areas, for towns and cities are notably rich in such local resources.

As U.S. forces become increasingly digitized and reliant on commercial off-the-shelf (COTS) products, the list of reportable facilities should reflect the change. Since many of the systems are COTS computers or related components, good IPB analysis will include the identification of computer retailers and repair capabilities within the urban AO. Knowledge of such resources will help warfighters needing to quickly replace a laptop computer or another otherwise readily unavailable component with an off-the-shelf substitute.

Innovative urban requirements like these should influence the design of unit training. This preparation might include developing and practicing drills that have never before been incorporated in SOPs or manuals. Methods of rapidly recovering, moving, or destroying vehicles along narrow streets or in other constricted places require development, testing, and refinement. Resultant ad hoc or design modifications to vehicles should be consciously distributed to those with a possible interest, so that all affected parties can take advantage of the initiatives (as should failed efforts, to keep other organizations from repeating them). Changes can be dramatic in effect (e.g., resulting in the incorporation of a neutral steer capability in Stryker vehicles or adapting Abrams tanks as CSS transport and medical evacuation vehicles).[6] They might be subtle (replacing some of a truck's cargo capacity with repair parts and equipment so that every truck can support BDAR in the field). Only with the foresight gained via such preliminary field experimentation, whether at training centers, schools, or elsewhere, will CSS units be able to appropriately respond to the rapidly changing needs and unique hazards of urban battlegrounds.

Means for making requirements known and disseminating them to appropriate individuals for consideration are called for. The Center for Army Lessons Learned would logically be a primary player in this initiative, as would CSS headquarters at every echelon. Project managers should not only be recipients of such information. They should also strive to maintain awareness of both evolving tactical demands and promising technological developments that could favorably influence the development of their own and other systems. It is crucial that timeliness be a defining characteristic regardless of the procedures employed in such an information exchange. Bureaucratic inertia will otherwise tend to ensure that innovations distantly lag field requirements and technological possibilities.

---

[6]"Neutral steer" means that the vehicle can turn within its own body length by rotating the tracks (or tires) on opposing sides of the system in opposite directions. The benefits include not having to back up (as there might be insufficient space to do so or a danger of striking noncombatants), speed in reversing direction, and a considerable intimidation factor as opposed to jockeying the system back and forth several times in a tight space.

Chapter Seven

OTHER

LIAISON

> Maneuver sustainment is all about exploiting information, credible
> and effective sources of support, relationships, and speed of com-
> mand to maximize combat power. Speed of command is defined
> as the time it takes to recognize and understand a situation, iden-
> tify and assess options, select a Course of Action (COA), and trans-
> late it into actionable orders.
>
> TRADOC Pam 525-4-0, *The United States Army Objective Force*
> *Maneuver Sustainment Support Concept*, 2001

Australian leaders overseeing multinational operations in Dili, East
Timor, found that understanding between coalition members was
sometimes poor despite thorough briefings by the Australian headquarters. They found that the problem was one of language, not un-
common when various countries come together to support military
undertakings. Concerns in this regard are especially applicable when
operations include large urban areas, for the density of forces needed
means that many units are likely to be in close proximity. Whereas
various nations' representatives might have only occasional contact
with those speaking other languages in a more open area of operations, in a city many will be within small arms range of each other.
This density means that liaison and detailed coordination will be
essential to successful completion of even the most routine tasks.
Lack of effective communication can endanger friendly force soldiers' lives, threaten successful interactions with local civilians, and
undermine the chances of accomplishing assigned missions. These

difficulties are magnified by a military culture's unique terminology within its personnel's native language. Even U.S. service personnel at times find it difficult to understand the acronyms or phrases used in other American arms. The problem is exacerbated when the specialized terminology has a technical character, as will often be the case in the CSS field. It is therefore not surprising that members of various militaries have difficulty understanding discussions even if their command of English is excellent. Unless those individuals have had the opportunity to study at a U.S. service school, chances are that their second-language skills are based on what was learned in civilian education programs that did not cover military terminology. Returning to the example of Dili, an Australian officer recalled that

> Three Thai colonels interviewed in Dili [concluded] that "the basic problem is language—we don't always understand what you are saying in English." They estimated that the Asian officers, in particular, understood only half of what was said in briefings and conferences, and they believed that Australian officers giving briefings appeared unaware of the issue. The colonels pointed out that the method of briefing needs to be adjusted to the audience, and that Australian officers tended to focus on the message and not on "reading" their audience. Their suggestions included reducing jargon, paying more attention to the level of comprehension exhibited by non-English speakers, and slowing down the presentations. This last point was of particular importance at the end of the briefings when questions were solicited. The rapid pace at which Australian briefings were "wrapped up" posed major problems for the Asian officers. They were still formulating questions.[1]

The author went on to observe that "there is a distinct need for more linguists to facilitate understanding between coalitions—not only at the strategic and tactical levels, but in the all-important area of logistics."[2] His observation will hold all the more true if various nations agree to pool resources so as to reduce the amount of materiel that must be imported into a theater by each.

---

[1] Ryan, *Primary Responsibilities,* p. 92.

[2] Ibid., p. 106.

EXPLOSIVE ORDNANCE DISPOSAL (EOD)

Currently EOD assets are part of a corps support or theater support command structure. The lack of explosive ordnance expertise could prove problematic in urban environments. Unexploded ordnance is especially troublesome in densely populated built-up areas. The possibility of imminent injury or death is far greater due to the sheer number of potential victims. The myriad rooftops, streets, patios, playgrounds, and other surfaces on which munitions can land make detection difficult. That some ordnance will likely remain for weeks or months after urban combat means that an effective and sustained education campaign, one involving both the indigenous citizenry and government authorities, will be necessary. Unexploded munitions in Safwon, southeastern Iraq, were a concern after the cessation of Persian Gulf War hostilities in 1991. U.S. forces waged a synchronized information operations and EOD campaign in an effort to stop Iraqi children and other civilians from harming themselves by picking up dangerous friendly force ordnance. Figure 7 is a poster that was used to warn members of the urban population about the dangers of ordnance. (The issue continues to be one of concern. Unexploded ordnance likewise caused a number of civilian casualties in Iraqi urban areas after the 2003 conflict.)

Cramped spaces, ordnance concealed amidst trash and other debris, and the potential for hair-trigger sensitivity after munitions reflect off of hard surfaces make EOD especially dangerous for those tasked with the job of neutralizing this refuse of war in a built-up area. Unmanned ground vehicles offer a less dangerous way to move or neutralize dangerous munitions. One is the TALON robot, a modular system that uses a removable, double-jointed device with a pincer arm for EOD operations.[3] TALON is an all-weather platform with day and night capability, controlled through a fiber optic link from a briefcase-sized unit. A smaller version of the same type of system (called the SOLEM robot) is small enough to pass through checked baggage at an airport. Both systems are designed for use in urban environments. They can navigate steps, sewers, and tunnels. These and other robotic systems have considerable potential during urban

---

[3]Foster-Miller, "Man-Portable Robots for EOD Reconnaissance, communication, sensing and security," *http://www.army-technology.com/contractors/mines/foster/*.

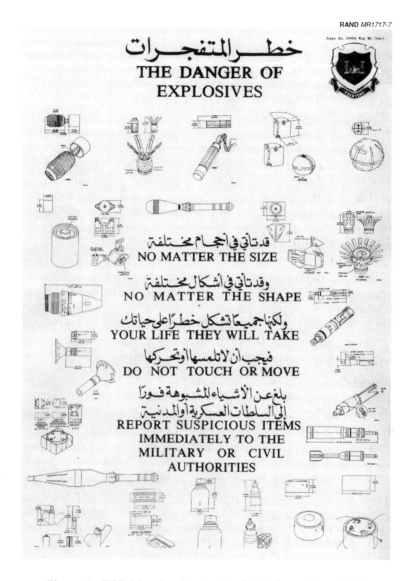

Figure 7—EOD Warning Poster Used in Safwon, Iraq, 1991

EOD operations that integrate their use with an educational campaign that makes procedures for reporting unexploded ordnance known, promulgates standards for appropriate ways to isolate a suspect site, and incorporates robots into EOD training and field procedures.

VEHICLE DESIGN

Current logistics vehicles are too often ill suited for operations in densely populated built-up areas. Despite its value as a troop carrier, evacuation vehicle, or at roadblocks when the threat level was low, the M113 armored personnel carrier (APC) was found by Americans fighting in 1989 Panama to dangerously expose the .50-caliber gunner to enemy fire from overhead or flank positions.[4] The APC's lack of protection against even small-caliber machine guns, much less rocket-propelled grenades (RPGs), led to an even more severe condemnation of the platform by the Israeli Defense Force (IDF). The Israelis flatly conclude that the M113 is not appropriate for combat. "It is an administrative vehicle . . . a taxi . . . to get us from one place to another."[5] The Israelis are considering replacement of their considerable M113 fleet with light amphibious vehicles (LAVs) but at the time of this writing are undecided. Notably, they do not consider the LAV an acceptable vehicle for urban combat operations either. LAVs are similarly deficient in their ability to protect vehicle occupants from larger-caliber weapons and the ubiquitous RPG found in virtually any force, state or nonstate, worldwide. Israelis instead rely on their Merkava tanks (which have a troop-carrying compartment) or APCs constructed from captured T55 tanks.

Actions in 1993 Mogadishu demonstrated that HMMWVs suffer even greater shortcomings. Vehicle gunners require protection not available due to the vehicle's design, and the driver and other passengers likewise have virtually nothing to protect them from even small arms fire without the addition of bulletproof glass and Kevlar protective blankets. All three of the above system types are also highly vulner-

[4]Operation Just Cause Lessons Learned, no page numbers.
[5]LtCol Ran, IDF, "IDF Lessons Learned Brief," briefing, Quantico, VA, June 10, 2002.

able to mines, one of the greatest vehicle killers in urban undertakings.

CSS providers in several countries have long called for truly armored vehicles (vice lightly armored systems such as the M113) to complement those that should remain in the relative safety of more rearward areas. The Israelis used their tanks in this role during urban operations in Lebanon and, as noted, continue to do so in Israel proper. Even the seemingly invincible Merkeva, which before February 2002 had never been destroyed by a guerrilla or terrorist force, suffered successful attacks by Palestinian irregulars four times in the two years thereafter.[6] The losses of so robust a system validate the need for more urban-capable supply, transport, medical evacuation, and maintenance vehicles. Ideal characteristics would include reduced vulnerability (if not invincibility) against up to RPG-type weapons, excellent mine protection, good visibility for crew and passengers, and a reasonable obstacle-breaching capability. A partial list of additional desirable performance specifications includes:

- A tight turning radius or neutral steer capability

- The ability to engage targets with lethal and nonlethal systems without exposure of weapon operators

- Smoke deployment

- An intimidating presence (valuable during support and stability operations)

- Difficult to climb onto and exterior components that are hard to remove

- Invulnerability to significant damage caused by flame, e.g., Molotov cocktails.

---

[6]The conditions under which these vehicles were destroyed reinforce the previous caution against relying on the same routes repeatedly during urban operations. Because of their invulnerability to RPGs, good thermal sights, and other characteristics, Merkava are used in a number of support roles, including resupply and aiding reactions to ambushes. Palestinians take advantage of routine, pattern, and knowledge of the limited number of routes that can support a tank's movement to bury improvised mines, command detonating them under their targets.

Potential future design characteristics in addition to those above could include enhancing vehicle stealth and providing self-inflating tires in nontracked variations.

Current design concepts for the Future Combat Systems (FCS) consider a family of fifteen different combat vehicles based upon a common platform. The efficiency of a common operating platform offers numerous CSS advantages in terms of reduced demands for maintenance training, personnel, and unique repair parts.

Unmanned vehicles, already mentioned in former discussions on casualty recovery and evacuation, could reduce or even eventually eliminate the need for armored systems (though use for medical evacuation would necessitate providing armor to at least the casualty compartment). Current initiatives include consideration of an unmanned ground vehicle (UGV) that performs reconnaissance and surveillance. Desirable capabilities would include an ability to breach doors; climb stairways or walls; clear obstacles; test enclosures for the presence of personnel, explosives, or other materials (e.g., traces of material signatures that reveal the presence of WMD); and navigate passageways in subterranean and above-ground infrastructures.

GENERAL ENGINEERING

> During most support operations and some stability operations, the focus of general engineering clearly supports and assists the urban population rather than sustains Army forces.
>
> FM 3-06, *Urban Operations*

The necessity of considering noncombatant needs has appeared repeatedly in the chapters above. U.S. forces will assume some responsibility for those trapped by the conflict even when the predominant objective is to defeat an enemy. There will also be missions in which support of indigenous civilians is the *raison d'être* for U.S. presence. A sampling of potential immediate general engineering-related needs on arrival in a theater of area of operations include:

- Provision of basic services essential for noncombatant survival, such as potable water, medical care, heat (should the weather be cold), and shelter

- Garbage removal and disposal

- Operational port and/or air facilities

- Repair of critical transportation infrastructure, e.g., bridges, roadways, and transport vehicles

- Flood control

There are others, some of which can take a military commander by surprise. A force going into a cold-weather area might require snow-removal capability. Indigenous firefighting and police services are at times inadequate or nonexistent.[7] Medical personnel deploying into theater during Operation Joint Endeavor found that the on-site crane was unable to unload essential x-ray and laboratory equipment, causing a day's delay in the availability of these critical resources.[8]

Such unusual general engineering requirements will demand more than equipment and operators. Urban environments come with their own sets of demands for even such seemingly straightforward operations as the above. Snow removal in rural areas demands little other than getting the unwanted covering off of a traveled roadway. In a city, vehicles, buildings, and other obstacles will interfere with snow removal by either directly blocking the route to be cleared or indirectly by requiring more than the simple movement of snow to the side of a street. Doing the latter would obstruct doorways, sidewalks, intersections, and alleys. Further, when the temperature rises, snowmelt would flow into basements or onto first floors. Fires can engulf hazardous materials in factories or warehouses, requiring civilian evacuation and safety precautions on the part of soldiers pressed into the role of firefighters. Such unusual responsibilities will require special expertise and training. Import of knowledgeable personnel or reliance on key publications will be essential. Both

---

[7]FM 3-06, p. 9-28.

[8]William T. Bester, *The Preparation and Deployment of the Initial Medical Force in Support of Operation Joint Endeavor,* Carlisle, PA: U.S. Army War College, 1998, pp. 16–17.

should be identified, and appropriate training conducted, prior to deployment. This preparation should include guides relied on by those in relevant fields in the United States. The *2000 Emergency Response Guidebook,* for example, provides guidance for fighting fires. In addition to addressing how to handle many specific types of blazes, it also tells participants what to do when the nature of the burning material is unknown. A general rule of thumb: the separation distance is sufficient if an individual is far enough away that he or she can put the entire incident behind a thumb.[9]

---

[9]Pat Easley, California Department of Forestry and Fire Protection, interview with Russell W. Glenn and Steven Hartman, Camarillo, CA, December 11, 2001.

Chapter Eight

SECURITY, FORCE PROTECTION, AND SAFETY

> The most important thing was to keep moving. One of the hardest things in the world to hit is a moving target.
>
> Mark Bowden, *Black Hawk Down*
> Mogadishu, Somalia, 1993

Urban areas come with security and force protection advantages and disadvantages for a CSS commander. Rarely will the abundance of all-around concealment be found elsewhere, concealment that may at times provide the additional benefit of significant cover from enemy fire. Nowhere else has as many indigenous sources of support, be they services, labor, equipment, or other resources. Built-up areas are more likely to have high-quality road surfaces, access to commercial communications capabilities, and proximity to air, sea, and land transportation hubs that facilitate rapid evacuation of injured and wounded. Local capabilities will most likely complement friendly force needs in many ways. Locals may be more familiar with indigenous diseases, for example. Towns or cities can offer power supply and lighting sufficient to constantly power or illuminate vital areas such as decontamination facilities, supply depots, and maintenance bays that keep soldiers from having to work while exposed to the elements.

Yet there will also be significant challenges. Security issues related to the presence of indigenous civilians, PVO and NGO representatives, and contract personnel have been mentioned. The density of buildings that block communications and GPS signal lines-of-sight also give enemy soldiers and thieves a means of closing on friendly force installations without being detected. The chaos of structures means that dismounted units as well as convoys will get lost, complicating CSS planning, increasing task completion times, and endangering those who might inadvertently enter booby-trapped, mined, or otherwise dangerous areas.

The character of threats is wide ranging, running the gamut from attack by enemy forces to demonstrations and riots to simple theft and disease. Indigenous groups posing these and other hazards often vary from those a military force expects to confront. They include irregular and paramilitary forces, organized criminal elements, militia, hostile police, those involved in the black market, and vandals.[1] Individuals and groups friendly at one point in time can later turn unfriendly. Even those with the best relations with friendly forces can suffer a change in attitude. For example, a demonstration by indigenous personnel employed on an American compound erupted in Mogadishu when U.S. forces announced reductions in the number of jobs.[2]

Even emerging U.S. Army force structures sometimes reflect little cognizance of the growing urban challenges that lie ahead. SBCT tactical operations centers (TOCs) are vehicle-mounted, predisposing them to set up in the open and thereby present considerable visual and noise signatures.[3] The urban locations capable of handling such large numbers of vehicles will most likely be quite limited, meaning that an enemy's IPB and reconnaissance efforts should have little trouble finding them. Noise signatures can possibly be reduced by relying on indigenous power supply, but access to sufficient outlets or sources within the immediate area of the TOC will be hard to find. Another means of providing power while suppressing audible signatures is to position generators within buildings. However, the structures will have to be well ventilated or soldiers will have to be kept out of them to avoid asphyxiation.

---

[1] FM 3-20.96 (2nd Coordinating Draft), p. 7-7 lists some of these threats.

[2] COL Stephen P. Hayward, *Personal Experience Monograph, DISCOM S-3, Somalia (29 Dec 92–25 Feb 93)*, Carlisle Barracks, PA: U.S. Army War College, 1998, enclosure "Commander's SITREP," 301800 Jan 93.

[3] Should structures sufficiently large to house entire TOCs, CSS or otherwise, exist, they would be prime targets for enemy analysts as they conduct their IPB.

CSS units in Mogadishu found that Class IV (construction and barrier materials) was in surprisingly short supply despite the many resources available in cities. Concertina wire, barbed wire, lumber, and pickets were among the materials lacking when the 10th Mountain Division sought to upgrade its force protection posture.[4] The burden is a double one for providers in such circumstances: not only do they lack the materials to protect themselves adequately, they also bear the responsibility to procure and bring forward what has to be imported from elsewhere. The problem can be overcome in part by taking advantage of innovative means of protecting installations. Ocean shipping containers, stacked to a desired height, have proved an effective protection from both observation and fires on several occasions. This asset may be readily available, as many cities of operational interest are near ports.

The IDF found that leaving CSS units in one place for too long increased their vulnerability to attack. They suggested a policy of frequent moves. Such displacements pose significant command and control challenges. Locations desirable for CSS operations will be limited. Supporting units need to remain within reasonable distance of those they support, further limiting the set of feasible locations. Movement will therefore mean a careful management of a limited number of acceptable facilities. Yet to simply shift units from one location to another, recently abandoned by some other organization, offers little in the way of force protection. The new unit is vulnerable to booby traps placed after the previous unit's departure and enemy attacks planned against those formerly occupying the site. CSS headquarters will have to assume responsibility for identifying desirable locations, assigning them to subordinate units, and providing a system for periodically moving the units assigned to them.

CONCLUDING REMARKS

The above-noted functional area challenges are but a sampling of what the CSS soldier will find confronting him in operations yet to come. Each urban environment will have its own unique individual and combination of demands for adaptation and innovation. Stay-

---

[4]Hayward, *Personal Experience Monograph,* enclosure "Commander's SITREP," 130600 Jan 93.

ing alert for such calls for change and communicating them to others will enhance operational effectiveness and survivability . . . if they are acted on. Cities are the most dynamic of ground force conflict environments. The force able to adapt effectively and in a timely fashion will reap considerable rewards. The force unable or unwilling to do so will very likely suffer in consequence.

Chapter Nine

CONCLUSION: THE UNENDING CALL TO PREPARE THE FORCE FOR URBAN OPERATIONS

> Urban combat is likely to be the most persistent of all forms of warfare.
>
> Michael Dewar
> *War in the Streets,* 1992

The authors admit to some frustration as they conclude this study. They are pleased to have had the opportunity to consider a topic long deserving of study. Yet their look has by necessity been but an initial overview. Individual functional areas received inaugural investigations only; each deserves more detailed analytical consideration. There are additional CSS concerns that remain virtually untouched. The determination of manpower attrition and class of supply consumption rates during urban operations, for example, will require extensive historical data mining and rigorous analysis of exercise results if planners are to have anything resembling reliable estimates on which to base their preparations for future urban operations. Thus this document should be considered a first step into a very important field of study rather than the final word, a foundation on which those responsible for future CSS urban operations can build rather than the ultimate product. Military leaders and trainers should encourage their subordinates at every level to contemplate, study, debate, write on, experiment with, and apply innovations, adaptations, and even the occasional seemingly bizarre concept in the ever-ongoing effort to enhance understanding and readiness. It is far easier to adapt from existing plans, doctrine, and standing operating procedures in times of crisis than create a capability from scratch. The mind in which a seed has been planted is more fertile ground for adjustments to new demands than one unperturbed by relevant thought.

Such considerations of the challenges that lie ahead will be the basis for creating and refining doctrine, tailoring training, guiding techno-logical development, and adapting force structure. It is sometimes the small things that determine the difference between mission suc-cess and failure: driver training emphasizing how to react under fire during an ambush, selecting routes that do not unnecessarily endan-ger indigenous children, spotting a behavior not in keeping with what the observant soldier has come to know as the norm are exam-ples. Training will therefore be fundamental to improved CSS urban readiness. Yet extant training facilities are far too small to incorpo-rate much more than the lowest echelons of combat units and per-haps a sampling of their supporting elements (or, as the case might be, CSS units and their supporting combat and combat support ele-ments). None is sufficient in size to permit a supporting unit to gain an appreciation for how difficult positioning and concealing large numbers of CSS vehicles and functions will be in a city. This con-straint must be taken as a given barring the (probably prohibitively costly) construction of an urban facility on a scale that dwarfs any-thing in existence or the securing of large expanses of abandoned or condemned built-up sites. Similarly, no urban simulation currently provides an acceptable training challenge for the American soldier. Innovation will be necessary, just as it is for combat and combat support units conducting urban exercises. Tactics, techniques, and procedures (TTP) will have to be conceived, tried, revised, perfected, and practiced at abandoned or condemned buildings on units' in-stallations or during urban terrain walks in nearby towns. CSS orga-nizations can integrate their leader training with that of maneuver units exercising at MOUT sites so that providers become more adept at relevant planning and coordination. There is no reason that those CSS leaders cannot occasionally secure such sites for their own use. Staff Judge Advocate officers found considerable value in experienc-ing first hand the unique demands of urban combat during training at Fort Knox's MOUT facility. Post-event comments reported that the experience was very beneficial and "a valuable template of how to better train soldier-lawyers."[1] Such initiatives are sparks for insightful debates and discussions within and beyond components of the CSS community.

The foregoing has cast light on a number of outstanding challenges. The objective in every case was to reveal ways to overcome these challenges rather than simply highlight their existence. Some hurdles are high ones, the result of years of ill-advised practice. The too-frequent separation of CSS and maneuver planning needs to end. Not only transporters and quartermasters, but medical, civil affairs, chaplain, and all other CSS warriors should be represented when pending operations are under consideration. Providers should conduct both their own command estimate and CSS IPB efforts while also being an integral part of those for the units they support, just as is the case with effective fire support, engineer, aviation, and other commanders and staff sections. The tempo of urban operations, the deluge of activity per unit time, is unforgiving of any but those with orchestrated plans and synchronized operations.[2]

It has been noted that the CSSC is not an organic component of the SBCT and that the Stryker Brigade Combat Team's ability to provide sufficient maintenance support for itself is therefore a significant concern. (Though it has also been noted that making the CSSC an organic part of the SBCT is under consideration, as are other corrective measures in this regard.)[3] CSS challenges of equivalent scope exist

---

[1]"CLAMO Note," *The Army Lawyer,* DA PAM 27-50-331, Charlottesville, VA: Center for Law and Military Operations (CLAMO), The Judge Advocate General's School, June 2000, p. 40.

[2]IPB is by character an anticipatory tool designed to allow a force to prepare for eventualities before they occur. As anticipation and adaptation are so critical during urban operations, staffs skilled in the use of IPB will have an advantage over those not employing such means of forecasting possible outcomes. As one way to gain an advantage is to impede the enemy's ability to adapt, there is also considerable potential in employment of IPB as a preemptive tool. For a discussion of IPB's use during urban operations, see Medby, *Street Smart.*

[3]FM 3-21.31 further discusses concerns about the need for CSSC support of the SBCT: "A key tenet of the concept of support is the capability to receive the combat service support company (CSSC) to augment the BSB to sustain the force after the initial stages of employment. Key constraints of the BSB include no capability to do scheduled maintenance, battle damage assessment and repair (BDAR/Class VII replacement only), field feeding, air medical evacuation, or EOD support. It also has only a limited distribution capability and minimal manning of the security, plans, and operations (SPO/distribution management) center (DMC), S6, and supply support

for other U.S. Army force structures. Armored and mechanized infantry divisions may lack the dismount strength to sufficiently secure their vehicles and other assets while also conducting noncombatant support, population control, or building clearing operations. Augmentation by light infantry (or, conversely, augmentation of light units by mechanized and armored assets) will therefore be necessary during future contingencies, much as it was in Hue and Mogadishu. Here too there are deficiencies in suitability for urban undertakings. The maintenance support needed by M1 and M2 vehicles is lacking in light units. Assignment of that support to the light unit by the heavier force could easily strain the latter's fixing capabilities given the likelihood that those vehicles will be allocated across a large number of infantry squads or platoons. Doctrine and force structures need to account for these light-heavy task organizations, and for urban operations in general, no less than is the case for the SBCT.

Concepts such as "soldier treat thyself" and vehicle "recover or lose" should spur debate and stimulate development of supporting doctrine if the choice is made to adopt them. Integration of PVOs and NGOs into coalitions would help to reduce noncombatant support requirements that a military force would otherwise have to assume, but the risks and political implications will undoubtedly cause controversy. Let the discussions begin. They need to start now. The requirements are already here.   Such proposals merit testing during experimentation to determine whether they truly warrant incorporation into service practice and to develop the guidelines necessary for that implementation. The debate and testing are themselves healthy. Modern urban areas are the most demanding of environments. Ignoring their terms poses considerable hazard to mission accomplishment and American lives.

---

activity (SSA). The austere design of the CSS structure is also insufficient to sustain the SBCT in garrison. The CSSC . . . is the *minimum* solution." M 3-21.31 (7-32), p. 10-30.

SUMMARY OF OBSERVATIONS AND RECOMMENDATIONS

This appendix provides a list of observations and recommendations discussed in greater detail in the report's main body. Readers should refer to that fuller coverage for expanded analysis of the elements listed and presentation of more specific subordinate considerations. The document's conclusion also contains additional observations.

Anticipation and Adaptation: Decentralization

- Frequent movement might be necessary to maintain effective security of smaller remote CSS activities.

- CSS soldiers' constant monitoring of the tactical situation, assessing risk, and deviating from plans when the situation demands will be necessary during urban actions.

- Deviations from table of organization and equipment (TOE) relationships or habitual task organizations might be necessary.

- Coalitions will at times find it effective to enter into agreements in which various coalition members agree to provide capabilities on a functional basis. Alternatively, nations can pool resources such as transportation assets and maintenance personnel, thereby reducing deployment requirements.

- The U.S. armed services would be well advised to include NGOs, PVOs, and commercial interests when planning and executing urban operations, especially as regards noncombatant support.

Anticipation and Adaptation: Centralization

- Keeping medics (or other similarly scarce resources) back and sending them forward only when needed will at times be advisable.

- CSS personnel will require frequent rest and rotation just as do those in maneuver units.

- Psychological operations (PSYOP) and deception efforts must be synchronized to include combat, combat support, combat service support, PVOs, NGOs, commercial interests, and other personnel as necessary. Intelligence collection and analysis similarly need to be centrally managed in a manner that best serves the needs of the entire force as well as its individual components.

Anticipation and Adaptation: Other Extraordinary Demands

- Some materials will have to be requisitioned and maintained in greater amounts to account for excessive urban wear and tear.

- CSS forces should be prepared to react to the sudden formation of civilian crowds.

- The CSS soldier will require training on how to avoid violating indigenous taboos.

- Maintain maximum flexibility during planning and execution.

- Preconfigure resupply loads and push them forward at every opportunity.

- Provide supplies to using units in required quantities as close as possible to the location where those supplies are needed.

- Protect supplies and CSS elements from the effects of enemy fire by both making use of cover and avoiding detection.

- Disperse and decentralize CSS elements with proper emphasis on communication, command and control, security, and proximity of main supply routes (MSR) for resupply.

- Plan for carrying parties and litter bearers.

- Plan for and use host country support and civil resources when practical.

- Position support units as far forward as the tactical situation permits.

- Plan for requesting and distributing special equipment such as body armor, toggle ropes with grappling hooks, ladders, and hand tools.

- Position support units near drop or landing zones (DZ/LZ) so that resupply involves the minimum necessary interim surface movement.

- Seek to cause the enemy to adapt improperly, too slowly, or not at all.

Integrate CSS C4ISR Operations with Others in the Force

- Train security personnel (to include guards), drivers, and other CSS personnel on how they can support intelligence collection and incorporate their input into a comprehensive HUMINT-collection system.

- Bureaucratic and organizational stovepipes should not be allowed to impede innovators' assumption of a systemic (macro) problem-solving perspective.[1]

- Leader training and doctrine should account for the possibility of CSS officers leading operations, notably during support or stability operations.

- Requisite combat, combat support, and combat service support unit communications; training, and equipment need to be compatible.

- Decisions that affect local conditions and the political situation will require evaluation from a common perspective.

- Combat service support elements need to have the same maps, overhead imagery, and communications capabilities as do other arms. In the absence of maps with appropriate scales, overhead photos or other imagery will be called for. Gridlines and graphi-

---

[1]Further discussion of this point and examples appear in the chapter on manning issues (in particular, those related to medical adaptation and anticipation).

cal information added to the raw products must be consistent across all branches and units.

- CSS leaders should contemplate how their units (systems) will influence and be affected by systems in the urban environment in which they operate.

- CSS planners should consider how they might work to preclude the inflation that their forces, PVOs, NGOs, and other outsiders will introduce by independently competing for indigenous resources rather than cooperatively agreeing to a pricing scheme.

- Properly selecting the point in time at which to begin transitioning from shipments of combat-specific materiel and personnel to those that will be in demand after the fighting has stopped will greatly impact urban population suffering and (potentially) worldwide perceptions of an operation's success.

- Include consideration of the second- and higher-order effects of decisions or actions.

- Those making pre-operation estimates should not unthinkingly rely on what little historical consumption data is available. ROE and many other factors will influence consumption.

Extraordinary CSS Demands During Urban Operations

- U.S. Army doctrine recommends that logisticians plan for ammunition usage at four times normal consumption rates.

- The mix of ammunition types demanded by urban missions are likely to differ considerably from that found in most other environments.

- More widespread development and fielding of binary munitions (made up of two components that are inert until brought together) is desirable.

- CSS personnel will have to be prepared to transport and supply nonlethal systems, maintain relevant equipment, and clean up areas when the effects are no longer needed. It is also likely that support units will find it beneficial to employ nonlethal capabilities themselves as they defend storage facilities, protect convoys, or otherwise find a need to influence noncombatant behavior. Proper training in their use will therefore be necessary.

- Properly treating those with wounds from nonlethal weapons might require specialized training. U.S., coalition, and indigenous medical personnel should be properly informed and, as appropriate, trained in this regard.

- As nonlethal capabilities enter service inventories in increasing numbers, CSS leaders should prepare for the second- and higher-order effects these systems will have on operations.

- Due to the many responsibilities CSS units will have with respect to nonlethal systems, it would benefit support soldiers were their leaders to take an active role in these capabilities' development and acquisition.

- Commanders should consider predeployment garrison training during which their soldiers carry personal weapons loaded with blanks.

- Leaders have a similar responsibility to ensure that their soldiers are well trained on the implications involved in employing nonlethal systems. This training should go well beyond simple operation of the weapon to encompass:

  — Likely reactions by those targeted (to include the possibility that they might respond to what they believe is lethal fire).

  — System effects on innocents inadvertently affected within the area influenced.

  — Appropriate ROE for the use of such capabilities.

  — The legal implications of employing the systems, to include deliberately targeting noncombatants or knowingly including them in the group targeted.

  — Appropriately task organizing lethal and nonlethal capabilities for soldier protection.

MANNING ISSUES

Medical Adaptation and Anticipation

- Urban operations will require more relief for stretcher-bearers and other CSS soldiers.

- The mix of medical specialists deployed during urban operations should account for the different mix of wounds and other medical ailments found during urban operations.

- Changes, perhaps something as straightforward as creation of a buddy system, can help to mitigate the problem of sometimes not being able to determine the location of casualties.

- Casualty self-treatment ("Soldier, treat thyself") might be advisable in lieu of sending personnel to provide immediate attention to wounded, at least in those cases in which the prospective patient is able to render such self-aid. Training, including how to forestall the onset of shock in oneself, will be critical to the success of such an adaptation.

- Ad hoc means of recovery and evacuation should not be overlooked (e.g., using an armored vehicle as a screen, employing smoke, or shining blinding lights toward an enemy at night).

- Move medical care closer to the wounded.

- Adding to the number of combat lifesavers in units is another way to increase the quality of care forward. Similarly, increasing the number of medics is desirable.

- A controversial but potentially very valuable further step would be upgrading the skills required of medics.

- Technological innovation should be considered in the medical realm as for any other.

- Anticipation and adaptation during concept development and equipment procurement should be as much a part of improving urban capabilities as are battlefield adjustments.

- CSS planners should not overlook the use of indigenous health services in treating U.S. or other coalition member nations' soldiers.

- Changes in types of wounds will influence the mix of medical specialties brought into a theater; they should also affect the training that medical personnel at every echelon receive prior to deploying.

- Just as a maneuver unit trains to conduct its tasks in body armor, medical personnel need to train for the types of wounds expected in a force wearing protective vests.

- Training should also account for a relative increase in secondary munition effects and casualties caused by soldiers stumbling over building debris.

- Training medics and engineers on how to properly remove rubble that has fallen on a man so as not to increase the extent of his injuries is essential when urban operations are likely, as is recognizing the symptoms of internal injuries due to crushing or compression. It is the more so when an adversary has a thermobaric weapons capability. Medical training should include telling personnel to look at the area around the wounded soldier for telltale signs of a thermobaric attack or asking others in the vicinity whether they know how the injury occurred. Training for treating suspected overpressure victims should include the following guidance:

  — Introduce IVs with caution. The introduction of fluid can worsen a casualty's condition due to lung damage. However, injury to the spleen and other organs will likely require the infusion of these same fluids.

  — Be prepared to provide ventilatory support forward on the battlefield and to do so within six to eight hours of injury.

  — The condition of the patient will most likely mean that medical evacuation by the fastest feasible means is desirable. However, damage to lungs—and the possibility that the changes in atmospheric pressure experienced during air evacuation might exacerbate that damage—could call for alternative means of evacuation from medical points in the rear. In such cases, it is advisable not to air evacuate without preparing the patient for life-threatening problems en route (barotrauma).

- — Do not consider the casualty a "walking wounded" even if he is initially able to walk.

- — Examine the eardrums. (Note, however, that field medics currently have no means to do so other than looking at the exterior of the ear.)

- The extreme physiological and mental demands associated with urban operations will require physical training before, changes in support during, and a readiness to address consequences after actions.

- Increase caloric intake during urban operations.

- Longer-term adaptations should include developing technological means of mitigating urban-related injuries.

- Vehicles employed for hauling materials forward might be designated as ambulances or used in transporting remains on return trips.

- Being able to quickly retrofit one or more vehicle chassis types with a compact "mini aid station" would provide medical leaders with greater flexibility than having to rely on a lesser number of ambulances.

- Other potentially valuable medical or wound-related technological developments include:

  - — Capitalizing on the development of artificial plasma to reduce the cost of hemostatic bandages, or the general distribution of Quikclot artificial coagulant in individual first aid packets. (Note that USMC Quikclot use during the 2003 Gulf War had mixed results. More testing is advisable.)

  - — Protection for the groin, face, neck, and extremities similar to that currently available for the torso and head.

  - — Soldier location and status monitors.

Integrating CSS C4ISR Operations: Urban Medical Considerations

- NATO doctrine recommends equipping medical command vehicles with two radios, putting a radio in every ambulance, ensuring these systems are capable of secure communications, providing the medical community with GPS, and manning these organizations with sufficient communications personnel to sustain these systems during urban operations. However, U.S. experiments have shown that alternatives to simply increasing the number of radios, communicating in the clear, and burdening admin and logistics nets need to be found.

- Preventive medicine is notably important during urban operations.

- Heat injuries pose a danger during urban operations just as they do elsewhere.

- Proper training, early identification of symptoms, and effective treatment can all positively influence the numbers and extent of stress casualties.

- Urban terrain management puts special demands on leaders. Aid station locations should be given a high priority.

- Reconnaissance forces and CSS soldiers whose jobs allow them to see much of an area of operations need to know how to identify and report sightings of urban sites that meet aid station, hospital, and other provider needs.

Preparing for the Extraordinary: Medical Challenges

- Policies on the extent to which U.S. medical facilities will provide either routine or emergency care for allies need to be determined and made known early during operations in order to preclude avoidable negative repercussions and unrealistic expectations. The same is true of the degree to which noncombatant support will be provided.

- Interruptions in routine medical care can have dramatic effects on an urban population's health. Providing medical treatment to civilians, or facilitating that treatment by indigenous or PVO/NGO providers, could influence perceptions of mission success, save local noncombatants' lives, and reduce the chances of disease spread to U.S. personnel.

- Policies on medical care for noncombatants should be part of a conscious campaign that coordinates them with other forms of civil affairs (CA), PSYOP, and additional types of suasion in the service of identified friendly force objectives. Such a campaign would have to include consideration of how to avoid the negative consequences of the inevitable reduction or curtailing of such assistance.

- Handling of the dead demands a need for sensitivity to indigenous cultural norms.

Legal

- Commanders and those advising them will frequently find that "the host government" consists of more than a single entity or representative.

- American soldiers will have to know how to handle matters related to civilian labor, the protection of noncombatants, the division of authority between local police and themselves, acceptable reactions to criminal activities involving local civilians, and many other issues.

- Lawyers will be further challenged to define what is permissible so as not to unnecessarily constrain U.S. forces in their pursuit of mission accomplishment.

Finance

- Contracting for indigenous vehicle support, labor, and other necessities can (and should) influence the quantities and types of materiel and personnel brought into the theater.

- Coalition leaders should work with member nation militaries and, ideally, private and nongovernmental representatives and commercial interests (to include U.S. contractors) to fix prices or otherwise address the negative effects of price wars and disruption of the local economy.

SUSTAINING AND MOVING

General

- One way of speeding resupply, whether at top-off points or farther forward, is to preload magazines on ships or in rear areas rather than having the task done by forward field deployed CSS elements.

- Develop mission-specific strategic configured loads (SCL) for urban operations.

- Consider outsourcing the design, preparation, and depot-level storage of SCL.

- Precision airdrop capabilities may hold promise for urban operations resupply.

- Consider innovative air delivery and sea-based sustainment (on, over, and underwater systems) as means to complement other approaches to urban operations supply.

Fueling

- Innovative CSS leaders might be able to complement traditional refueling methods with several ad hoc initiatives given that urban areas are often locations in which large quantities of fuel are stored. Ports, airfields, and commercial petroleum-handling facilities can be designated as early targets for seizure, either to allow friendly forces to use the fuel on hand (after testing for suitability and modification as necessary) or for storage of imported petroleum, oil, and lubricant (POL) products.

- The vulnerability of fuel transporters and the difficulty of pulling combat vehicles sufficiently far back from the line of contact to reach those trucks means that innovations are likely to be called for to augment doctrinal means of replenishment.

- Urban CSS fuel sustainment operations might be well served by the use of available subterranean facilities.

- Widespread dispersion of fuel in an urban area will likely be desirable for security purposes. However, the current allocations of pump and hose assets for U.S. units will be insufficient should fuel storage and distribution nodes be so positioned.

- Experimentation is necessary to determine necessary pump capabilities, numbers of pumps, length of hose lines, and storage capacity needed to support each unit type.

- Increases in hose length requirements present an obvious argument for developing lighter and less bulky hoses.

- The following technologies might offer partial solutions to urban fuel distribution challenges:

  — The AAFARS refueling system (to distribute bulk fuel through a subterranean distribution system).

  — Undersea fuel bladders for both intermediate ship and ground vehicle refueling.

  — DMFD Mobile Fuel Mobility System mounted on a HMMWV.

Water

- As is the case with ammunition and casualty statistics, a lack of quality data on urban water consumption means that it will be difficult to gauge the appropriate balance between best guesses and quantities that overburden lift and indigenous capabilities.

- A means of supply superior to bottled water is necessary.

- Consider the use of subterranean infrastructure to produce and distribute bulk water.

Other

- Complete reliance on indigenous power supply exposes units to interruptions or coercion by those that control the source of such power. (The same is true of water supplies.) Plans should be in place to either replace local services/supplies if they are suspended, or to tailor operations to account for reduced amounts of indigenously supplied resources.

- Using armored vehicles for LOGPAC push offers increased survivability and force protection. Soft-skinned vehicles may be inadequate for the task, especially in environments in which the adversary has anti-tank weapons such as the RPG-7.

- Creating and prepositioning urban forward logistics elements (FLEs) to support critical points identified during CSS IPB analysis gives sustainers an additional means of enhancing operational responsiveness.

- Were sustainment based on resupply from a stationary FLE, a dismounted infantry leader would have to consider how to move supplies back to his fighting position with the minimum loss of fighting power.

- The size of "mouse holes," windows, or even some doorways can make it difficult if not impossible for soldiers to pass through these openings while wearing a full combat load.

- The SKEDCO litter or similar means can provide an innovative means of evacuating wounded or moving supplies.

- The rucksack is too large for MOUT operations.

- Testing is needed to determine daily caloric demands during urban contingencies, but evidence implies that meals designed to provide more sustenance per unit of food weight are called for.

- The larger numbers of nodes requiring CSS support combine with delays in turnaround times due to navigation difficulties, wear and tear on vehicles, and myriad other factors to make effective management of transport assets and supplies absolutely vital during urban operations.

- Maneuver units must not hoard haul capability.

- Soldiers will give up their own rations to relieve the suffering of those around them even when explicitly ordered not to do so.

- Planners who fail to compensate for longer transport times in built-up areas due to traffic density, lower speeds, narrow streets, difficulty of navigation, and other factors will find themselves chronically unable to meet their own timetables.

- Leaders and planners will need to vary routes used, designate alternate routes, specify secondary means of accomplishing sustainment tasks, and maintain flexibility in operations to deal with such events as nuclear, biological, and chemical attacks or public demonstrations.

- Tactical movement planners who do not coordinate with their CSS counterparts will find both maneuver and sustainment operations threatened with failure.

- Engineer units need to be assigned mobility responsibilities and locations at which they can preposition supporting equipment.

- CSS planners will have to work closely with their maneuver counterparts to assess risks and define the limits of the possible when planning transport of fighting vehicles and other mission requirements.

- Movement planners need to specify and coordinate routes for attack, withdrawal, reserve movement, replenishment, casualty and EPW evacuation, and movement of civilian refugees. They should in some, if not all, of these cases also incorporate alternate and secondary routes into plans.

- Chemlite consumption during urban operations is very high. Infrared chemlites are in particularly high demand.

- Infantrymen often desire the issue of M4 carbines in lieu of M16 rifles when fighting in cities.

- Means of breaking into rooms, through fences, or breaching other obstacles nonexplosively are needed for instances when noncombatants are in the area or explosives use is impractical.

- The density of civilians in urban areas means that a force's CSS capabilities might be insufficient to support the simultaneous conduct of large-scale support and combat operations.

- The presence of large numbers of indigenous females or very young children in the supported population could respectively influence the mix of hygiene or food products brought into a theater.

- Awareness of social norms before load planning could make the difference between public relations coup and unnecessary embarrassment.

- Units need to plan the destruction of supplies and equipment (other than medical) that cannot be evacuated.

FIXING THE FORCE DURING URBAN OPERATIONS

- Vehicles are threatened not only by direct fire from their front, rear, or sides and by mines underneath; engagement from upper stories and rooftops will be a constant threat.

- More frequent jarring against hard surfaces translates to more frequent calibration of equipment.

- Routine scheduled vehicle care will be vital in addition to aggressive PLL management and responsive emergency maintenance procedures.

- There is a need for deploying a robust maintenance capacity with any unit contemplating urban action.

- Timely situational awareness of a unit's equipment readiness posture, repair parts status, and maintenance support capabilities is essential to making the correct decisions that will allow it to maintain an appropriate operational tempo during urban operations.

- Maintaining responsiveness in providing battle damage assessment and repair (BDAR) and other fixing support means that CSS personnel will operate on contested terrain more frequently than is the norm.

- Having a means of hooking and dragging a disabled vehicle out of the way or positioning heavy vehicles in convoys such that they can ram those that are blocking progress is advisable.

- If a vehicle must be abandoned, operators should remove or destroy critical equipment.

- Rapidly repairing and returning systems to a fight will be crucial.

- Standard Army Maintenance System (SAMS) stock levels have to be checked to ensure they are sufficient for the higher attrition rates of urban operations. CSS managers should for similar reasons monitor stock levels for parts maintained exclusively by civilian contractors.

- Given the leanness of fixing forces often initially deployed to operations in urban centers, there is obvious value in prepositioning spares and repair materials and establishing depot facilities to which evacuated vehicles can be taken.

- CSS planners need to identify requirements for maintenance facilities during IPB analysis and bring them to the attention of any whose tasks involve travels through the area of operations.

- The list of reportable facilities should reflect the Army's increasing reliance on digitized and commercial-off-the-shelf (COTS) products.

- Innovative urban requirements should influence the design of unit training, conducted both prior to deployment and thereafter.

- It is worth embarking on a path toward developing vehicles and equipment that can be better tailored to suit the evolving needs of urban (and other types of) conflict.

OTHER CONSIDERATIONS (LIAISON, EOD, VEHICLE DESIGN, GENERAL ENGINEERING)

- There is a distinct need for more linguists to facilitate understanding between coalitions.

- Unexploded ordnance is especially troublesome in densely populated built-up areas.

- Current logistics vehicles are too often ill suited for operations in densely populated built-up areas.

- Unmanned vehicles, already mentioned in former discussions of casualty recovery and evacuation, could reduce or even eventually eliminate the need for armored systems.

- Personnel with critical general engineering expertise should be identified prior to deployment and given special training as required.

SECURITY, FORCE PROTECTION, AND SAFETY

- The IDF found that leaving CSS units in one place for too long increased their vulnerability to attack.

Books

Bowden, Mark, *Black Hawk Down: A Story of Modern War,* New York: Atlantic Monthly, 1999.

Briggs, Clarence E., *Operation Just Cause: Panama, December 1989, A Soldier's Eyewitness Account,* Harrisburg, PA: Stackpole, 1990.

Casper, Lawrence E., *Falcon Brigade, Combat and Command in Somalia and Haiti,* Boulder, CO: Lynne Rienner, 2001.

Dewar, Michael, *War in the Streets: The Story of Urban Combat from Calais to Khafji,* Newton Abbot, Devon: David and Charles, 1992.

Fenn, Elizabeth A., *Pox Americana: The Great Smallpox Epidemic of 1775–82,* New York: Hill and Wang, 2001.

Graves, Robert, *The Greek Myths: 1,* Baltimore: Penguin, 1968.

Heinl, Robert Debs, Jr., *Dictionary of Military and Naval Quotations,* Annapolis, MD: Naval Institute Press, 1985.

Heiser, Joseph M., Jr., *A Soldier Supporting Soldiers,* Washington, D.C.: Center of Military History, 1992.

Kern, Paul Bentley, *Ancient Siege Warfare,* Bloomington, IN: Indiana University Press, 1999.

Pagonis, William G., *Moving Mountains: Lessons in Leadership and Logistics from the Gulf War,* Boston: Harvard Business School Press, 1992.

Shulimson, Jack, et al., *U.S. Marines in Vietnam: The Defining Year, 1968,* Washington, D.C.: History and Museums Division, Headquarters, U.S. Marine Corps, 1997.

Thompson, Julian, *The Lifeblood of War Logistics in Armed Conflict,* London: Brassey's, 1991.

Articles

Alexander, Steven E., "Urban Warfare: U.S. Forces in Future Conflicts," *Military Review,* January–February 2002.

Armed Forces Information Service, "Electrified BDUs Definitely Aren't Your Father's Fatigues," *http://www.defenselink.mil/news/ Apr2002/n04082002_200204082.html,* accessed May 30, 2002.

Baillat, Jean-Michel, "Military Necessity Versus the Protection of the Wounded and Sick: A Critical Balance," *Military Medicine,* Vol. 167 (Supplement 3, 2002), pp. 1–19.

"Battlefield Repairs—Mobile Warfare," *The Economist,* April 13, 2002.

Baxter, Shannon, "Support Facilities for Hydrogen-Fueled Vehicles— Conceptual Design and Cost Analysis Study," *www.hydrogenus. com,* accessed February 13, 2002.

Brooke Ocean Technology, "ELSS Pod Posting," *http://www.brooke-ocean.com/elss-01.html,* accessed June 10, 2002.

Canadian Military Journal, "The Rebirth of Aerial Delivery, *http:// www.journal.forces.gc.ca/vol2/no1_e/logistics_e/logistics1_e.html,* accessed May 14, 2002.

Center for Army Lessons Learned, "Urban Combat Operations: Appendix F: Simple Marking Devices," *http://call.army.mil/products/ newsltrs/99-16/appendf.htm,* accessed June 18, 2002.

Center for Army Lessons Learned, "Urban Combat Operations; Chapter 9: Flight Operations in Urban Areas," *http://call.army.mil/products/newsltrs/99-16/chap9.htm*, accessed June 18, 2002.

Department of Energy, "Hydrogen: The Fuel for the Future," DOE/GO-10095-099, DE95004024, March 1995.

Dunn, Andrew C., "East Timor: The Work of the New Zealand Forward Surgical Team from 1999 to 2000," *Military Medicine*, Vol. 167 (October 2002), pp. 810–811.

Durante, Arthur A., "Simple Marking Devices for Urban Operations," *http://www.call.army.mil/products/newsltrs/99-16/appendf.htm*, accessed June 18, 2002.

FAS Organization, "SEAL Delivery Vehicle (SDV) Advanced SEAL Delivery System," *http://www.fas.org/irp/program/collect/seal_sdv.htm*, accessed June 10, 2002.

Faversham House Group Ltd 2001, "Military Has Keen Interest in Fuel Cell Technology," *http://www.climateark.org/articles/2001/3rd/mishaskee.htm*, accessed March 28, 2002.

Ferry, Charles P., "Mogadishu, October 1993: A Company XO's Notes on Lessons Learned," *Infantry* (September–October 1994), authors' copy was USACGSC reprint with page numbers 6-39 to 6-49.

Fiskum, Ronald J., "Fuel Cell Summit," *http://www.pnl.gov/fuel cells.htm*, accessed March 28, 2002.

Ginsburg, Janet, "Hydrogen Cars May Hit Showrooms by 2005," *http://news.nationalgeographic.com/news/2001/10/1016_TVhyperca r.html*, accessed February 13, 2002.

Grau, Lester W., and Timothy Smith, "A 'Crushing' Victory: Fuel-Air Explosives and Grozny 2000," *http://call.army.mil/fmso/fmsopubs/issues/fuelair/fuelair.htm*, accessed November 19, 2001.

Grau, Lester W., and Timothy L. Thomas, "'Soft Log' and Concrete Canyons: Russian Urban Combat Logistics in Grozny," *http://fmso.leavenworth.army.mil/fmsopubs/issues/softlog/softlog.htm*, accessed September 15, 2003.

Harris, James, "My Two Wars," *The New York Times,* April 20, 2003, p. 8.

Holcomb, John, et al., "Efficacy of a Dry Fibrin Sealant Dressing for Hemorrhage Control After Ballistic Injury," *Journal of Special Operations Medicine,* Vol. 1 (Fall 2001), pp. 4–5.

"How to Save 1m Children a Year," *The Economist,* Vol. 364 (July 6, 2002), p. 80.

Mabry, Robert L., et al., "United States Army Rangers in Somalia: An Analysis of Combat Casualties on an Urban Battlefield," *Journal of Special Operations Medicine,* Vol. 1 (Fall 2001), pp. 24–40.

Military Analysis Network, "Landing Craft, Air Cushion," *http://www.fas.org/man/dod-101/sys/ship/lcac.htm*, accessed June 14, 2002.

"Military Interested in Fuel Cells for Fighting," Gannett News Service, *http://seattletimes.nwsource.com/news/nation-world/html98/mill31_20000331.html*, accessed March 28, 2002.

Parker, Phillip, "Somalia Update: Military Operations on Urbanized Terrain (MOUT)," *http://call.army.mil/products/nftf/nftf1293/prt5.htm*, accessed March 14, 2002.

Pike, John, "FATHAWK/WETHAWK Remote, Rearm, and Refuel Deployable Distribution System," *http://www.fas.org/man/dod-101/sys/ac/equip/wethawk.htm*, accessed March 28, 2002.

PM Paws, "Advanced Aviation Forward Area Refueling System," *http://www.tacom.army.mil/dsa/pmtaws/pm_paws.htm*, accessed 2002.

Reid, Harry, "Why Hydrogen? Ten Reasons Why the United States Should Switch to a Hydrogen Energy Economy," *www.ttcorp.com/nha/why_reid.htm*, accessed February 13, 2002.

Ritchie, Elspeth C., and Robert Mott, "Caring for Civilians During Peace Keeping Missions: Priorities and Decisions," *Military Medicine,* Vol. 167 (Supplement 3, 2002), pp. 14–16.

Scripps News Service, "Hold the Lettuce: Nutrition Patches in Soldiers' Future," *http://www.thedailycamera.com/science/science/20apatc.html*, accessed May 30, 2002.

United States Advanced Ceramics Association, "What Are Advanced Ceramics," *http://www.advancedceramics.org/index.htm*, accessed March 28, 2002.

White, S.R., N.R. Sottos, P.H. Geubelle, J.S. Moore, M.R. Kessler, S.R. Sriram, E.N. Brown, and S. Viswanathan "Autonomic Healing of Polymer Composites," *Nature,* Vol. 409 (2001), pp. 794–797, *http://www.ssm7.aae.uiuc.edu/self-healing/publications.html,* accessed October 18, 2002.

Xiangxu Chen, Matheus A. Dam, Kanji Ono, Ajit Mal, Hongbin Shen, Steven R. Nutt, Kevin Sheran, and Fred Wudl, "A Thermally Remendable Cross-linked Polymeric Material," *Science* (March 1, 2002), http://www.sciencemag.org, accessed October 16, 2002`

Reports, Manuals, and Monographs

"Abrams Urban Quick Reference Guide," Publication Number ST 3-20.12-1, U.S. Army Training and Doctrine Command, December 2002.

Bester, William T., *The Preparation and Deployment of the Initial Medical Force in Support of Operation Joint Endeavor,* Carlisle, PA: U.S. Army War College, 1998.

Butler, Frank K., and John H. Hagmann (eds.), *Tactical Management of Urban Warfare Casualties in Special Operations,* proceedings from panel conducted by the Special Operations Medical Association, Tampa, FL, December 7, 1998.

Cecchine, Gary, et al., *Army Medical Strategy: Issues for the Future,* Santa Monica, CA: RAND, 2001.

Combat Service Support, FM 3-06.11, Chapter 13, *http://155.217.58/cgi-bin/atdl.dll/fm/3-06.11/ch13.htm.*

Combined Arms Operations in Urban Terrain, FM 3-06.11, February 28, 2002, downloaded from *http://155.217.58.58/cgi-bin/atdl.dll/fm/ 3.06.11/toc.htm.*

Defense Technology Objectives for the Joint Warfighting Science and Technology Plan and the Defense Technology Area Plan, Department of Defense, February 2002.

Delk, James, "MOUT: A Domestic Case Study—The 1992 Los Angeles Riots," in Russell W. Glenn et al. (eds.), *The City's Many Faces: Proceedings of the RAND Arroyo-MCWL-J8 UWG Urban Operations Conference,* Santa Monica, CA: RAND, 2000, pp. 79–156.

Doctrine for Joint Urban Operations, Joint Publication 3-06, Washington, D.C.: Office of the Joint Chiefs of Staff, September 16, 2002.

Doctrine for Joint Urban Operations, Joint Publication 3-06 (Final Coordination Draft), Washington, D.C.: Office of the Joint Chiefs of Staff, February 20, 2002.

Explosive Ordnance Disposal and Unit Operations, FM 9-15.

Fighting in Built-Up Areas (FIBUA) [Objectif Doctrine: L'Engagement des forces Terrestres en Zone Urbanisee], Commandement de la Doctrine et de L'Enseignement Militaire Superieur de L'Armee de Terre (bilingual edition), undated. Received by author in 2002 during a visit to Canadian Armed Forces Staff College.

Galbraith, William S., "Analysis of Logistics Sustainment in Urban Operations: The Need for Combat Service Support NCO and Officer Training Centers to Implement Instruction Reflecting Sustainment in Urban Operations," LEDC course paper, Class 02-001.

Gbur, Charles J., "Battalion Aid Station Support of Military Operations in Urban Terrain (BASS MOUT)," paper by battalion surgeon for the 3rd Battalion, 25th Marines Reserve battalion aid station, undated.

Glenn, Russell W., et al., *Honing the Keys to the City: Refining the United States Marine Corps Reconnaissance Force for Urban Ground Combat Operations,* Santa Monica, CA: RAND, 2003.

Glenn, Russell W., *Visualizing the Elephant: Managing Complexity During Military Urban Operations,* Santa Monica, CA: RAND, DB-430-A, 2003.

Hambric, Harry N., "The Antipersonnel Mine Threat," Fort Belvoir, VA: Humanitarian Demining Project, Night Vision Electronic Sensors Directorate, undated.

Hayward, COL Stephen P., *Personal Experience Monograph, DISCOM S-3, Somalia (29 Dec 92–25 Feb 93),* Carlisle Barracks, PA: U.S. Army War College, 1998.

Holcomb, John, "The Urban Area During Support Missions: Case Study Mogadishu," in Russell W. Glenn (ed.), *Capital Preservation: Preparing for Urban Combat in the Twenty-first Century,* Santa Monica, CA: RAND, 2001.

Hydrogen: The Fuel for the Future, Department of Energy, DOW/GO-10095-099, DE95004024, March 1995.

Improving Land Armaments: Lessons from the Balkans, RTO-TR-AC/323(SAS-041)TP/, Brussels, Belgium: North Atlantic Treaty Organization, November 2001.

The Interim Brigade Combat Team, FM 3-21.31 (7-32) (Draft), Fort Benning, GA: U.S. Army, July 10, 2001.

Joint Warfighting Science and Technology Plan, Department of Defense, February 2002.

Keating, Edward G., *Compensating Civilians on the Battlefield,* Santa Monica, CA: RAND, 1993.

Lee, Mark A., *A Curious Void: Army Doctrine and Toxic Industrial Materials in the Urban Battlespace,* Fort Leavenworth, KS: School of Advanced Military Studies monograph, January 2, 2001.

Mackey, Robert R., *Building a Shallow Army: Replacement Operations in the Future Force,* Fort Leavenworth, KS: School of Advanced Military Studies, 2002.

Medby, Jamison Jo, and Russell W. Glenn, *Street Smart: Intelligence Preparation of the Battlefield for Urban Operations,* Santa Monica, CA: RAND, 2002.

Military Capabilities—Focused Attention Needed to Prepare US Forces for Combat in Urban Areas, General Accounting Office Report, February 25, 2000.

Military Operations in Urbanized Terrain, MCWP 3-35.3.

Operation Just Cause Lessons Learned: Volume III-Intelligence, Logistics, & Equipment, Fort Leavenworth, KS: U.S. Army Center for Lessons Learned, October 1990.

"Precision Airdrop Distribution Concept of Support for Future Military Operations," briefing charts and product description provided by Ed Doucette, U.S. Army Natick Soldier Center, accessed May 14, 2002.

RSTA Squadron, FM 3-20.96 (2nd Coordinating Draft), U.S. Army Armor Center, June 12, 2001.

Ryan, Alan, *Primary Responsibilities and Primary Risks: Australian Defense Force Participation in the International Force East Timor,* Australian Land Warfare Studies Centre Study Paper No. 304, November 2000.

Schneck, William C., *Landmines Versus Vehicles (1st Revision),* Fort Belvoir, VA, Countermine Division, Night Vision Electronic Sensor Directorate, undated.

"The Threat from Blast Weapons," *The Bulletin For Soldiers by Soldiers,* Canadian Army Lessons Learned Centre, Vol. 7, No. 3, January 2001.

The Stryker Brigade Combat Team, FM 3-21.31, Washington, D.C.: Headquarters, Department of the Army, March 13, 2003.

United States Army, *An Infantryman's Guide to Combat in Built-Up Areas,* with Change 1, FM 90-10-1 (redesignated FM 90-10.11), October 3, 1995, G-5, accessed at *http://www.globalsecurity.org/military/library/policy/army/fm/90-10-1/appg.pdf,* October 1, 2002.

United States Army, *Mission Support Training Plan for the Brigade Support Medical Company,* ARTEP 8-108F-30-MTP (Working Draft), Appendix F, "Threat Environment (Medical Units)," February 3, 2002.

United States Army, *The United States Army Objective Force Maneuver Sustainment Support Concept,* TRADOC Pamphlet 525-4-0,

Fort Monroe, VA: U.S. Army Training and Doctrine Command, December 3, 2001.

Urban Generic Information Requirements Handbook (GIRH), MCIA-1586-005-99, Quantico, VA: U.S. Marine Corps, December 1998. (This document is For Official Use Only).

Urban Operations, FM 3-06 (90-10) (Drag edition), Washington, D.C.: Headquarters, Department of the Army, May 20, 2002.

Urban Warfare Logistics (UWL): Study and Analysis, Final Report, U.S. Army Logistics Integration Agency, April 19, 1999.

Waters, Henry J., "The Medical Implications of Combat in Cities," Student Research Paper, Fort Leavenworth, KS: Command and General Staff College, January 10, 1975.

Weiss, Jack L., *Personal Experience Monograph: Supporting the Quick Reaction Force in Somalia—Operation Continue Hope/ Somalia,* July 1993–February 1994, Carlisle, PA: U.S. Army War College, 1996.

Wilson, Mahlon S., and Christine Zawodzinski, *Small Battery—Fuel Cell Alternative Technology Development,* Los Alamos, NM: Los Alamos National Laboratory, 2001.

Interviews

Cancio, LTC Lee, telephone interview by Russell W. Glenn, February 12, 2003.

Darsch, Jerry, Department of Defense Combat Feeding Program, Natick Soldiers Systems Center, telephone interview with Steven L. Hartman, October 4, 2002.

DeGay, Jean-Lewis, interview with Russell W. Glenn, Natick, MA, May 2, 2003.

DeRoche, Larry M., interview with Russell W. Glenn, Fort Lewis, WA, November 28, 2002.

Doucette, Edward, Airdrop/Aerial Delivery Directorate, U.S. Army Natick Soldier Center, telephone interview with Steve Hartman, May 14, 2002.

DCD-QM, telephone interview with Steven Hartman, March 6, 2003.

Dumond, John, RAND, interview with Russell W. Glenn and Steven L. Hartman, Santa Monica, CA, December 20, 2001.

Easley, Pat, California Department of Forestry and Fire Protection, interview with Russell W. Glenn and Steven L. Hartman, Camarillo, CA, December 11, 2001.

Fifth Special Forces Group representatives, interview with Russell W. Glenn, Tampa, FL, September 19, 2002.

Gellert, LTC (USA) Frederick, interview with Russell W. Glenn, Fort Lewis, WA, November 28, 2002.

Howard, Doug. U.S. Army Mortuary Affairs Center (MAC), interview with Russell W. Glenn, Fort Lee, VA, July 31, 2002.

Karen, BG Arye (IDF, ret.), interview with Russell W. Glenn, Ashkelon, Israel, February 17, 2002.

Modrow, Harold E., Special Assistant, U.S. Army Medical Materiel Development Activity (USAMMDA) with responsibility for homeostatic dressing programs, telephone interview with Russell W. Glenn, April 9, 2002,.

Owens, LTC Kevin C., battalion commander for the 2/75th Ranger Battalion, 1SG Michael T. Kennedy, and 1SG Brendon Durkan, interview with Russell W. Glenn, Fort Lewis, WA, November 29, 2001.

Purdue, William, interview with Steven Hartman, Fort Lee, VA, April 17, 2002.

Shamni, BG (IDF) Gadi, Head of Israeli Defense Force Infantry and Paratrooper Doctrine, interview with Russell W. Glenn, Adam Training Area, Israel, February 18, 2002.

Special Forces briefing on operations in Afghanistan, McDill Air Force Base, Tampa, FL, September 19, 2002.

Thompson, LTC (USA) Dennis M., interview with Russell W. Glenn, Fort Lewis, WA, November 28, 2002.

Zaken, BG (IDF, ret.) Nachum, Battalion Commander, 433 Armored Battalion, Armored Brigade #500 during 1973 fighting in Suez City, interview with Russell W. Glenn, Latrun, Israel, April 10, 2000.

Briefings, Emails, and Miscellaneous Sources

"Achieving Transformation, 2002–2010," Handout provided at the CASCOM Senior Commanders Conference, May 22–23, 2002, Richmond, VA.

"Armor-Infantry Integration at JRTC," briefing presented at the 16th Cavalry Squadron Urban Operations Conference, Fort Knox, KY, September 10, 2002.

Army Regulation 40-25, "Nutrition Standards and Education," Washington, D.C.: Headquarters, Departments of the Army, Navy, and Air Force, June 15, 2001.

Arquilla, John, and David Ronfeldt, *Swarming and The Future of Conflict*, Santa Monica, CA: RAND, DB-311-OSD, 2000.

"Assault Hoseline System (AHS), PM Petroleum and Water Systems (PAWS)," *http://peocscss.tacom.army.mil/pmFP/pm_paws/systems/ahs.htm,* accessed October 18, 2002.

Born, Kevin, email to Russell W. Glenn, "Army countermine Capability Gaps," January 23, 2002.

Born, Kevin, email to Russell W. Glenn, "CSS Units Supporting Sustainment," November 9, 2001.

Born, Kevin, email to Steven L. Hartman, "Fuel in UO, Part II," April 16, 2002.

Born, Kevin, email to Russell W. Glenn, "Mountain & Urban Warfare," March 6, 2002.

Born, Kevin, email to Russell W. Glenn, "Updated CSS UO Study Comments," October 15, 2002.

Briggs, Jack, email to Russell W. Glenn, "Subject: HOOAH! Bar," May 20, 2003.

"CLAMO Note," *The Army Lawyer,* DA PAM 27-50-331, Charlottesville, VA: Center for Law and Military Operations (CLAMO), The Judge Advocate General's School, June 2000.

Cooper, Clay, "Military Operations Center (CMOC)," Fort Leavenworth, KS: Center for Army Lessons Learned, *News from the Front,* January–February 1997, *http://call.army.mil/products/nftf/janfeb97/civmil.htm,* accessed October 16, 2002.

Cosentino, Joseph, email and accompanying briefing slides forwarded to Russell W. Glenn, February 6, 2003.

"Current News: New Blood-Clotting Material May Revolutionize Combat First Aid," *http://www.mcwl.quantico.usmc.mil/active.html*; accessed July 16, 2002.

"D-Day Mobile Fuel Distribution System," Briefing provided by Mr. Buck Thomas, Naval Facilities Engineering Center, Point Hueneme, California; received via email to Steven L. Hartman, September 25, 2002.

"Executive Summary–Future Trends in Advanced Power Sources," a report prepared by the Canadian Military looking at future power source requirements and capabilities, 2002.

Gellert, Fred, email to Russell W. Glenn, "Fred Gellert's MOUT Trip Report," February 13, 2001.

Gerwehr, Scott, Russell W. Glenn, and Steven L. Hartman, "CSS Challenges in Future Urban Operations: Project Status," briefing given to U.S. Army Combined Arms Support Command representatives, Fort Lee, VA, January 16, 2002.

Glenn, Russell W., and Steven L. Hartman, "Urban CSS Operations: RAND Arroyo Urban CSS Project IPR," briefing given to U.S. Army Combined Arms Support Command representatives, Fort Lee, VA, April 18, 2002.

Harman, Larry, "Executive Summary of the Objective Force White Paper: The Expeditionary Support Force (ESF) and Maneuver

Sustainment Support (MSS)," Fort Lee, VA, CASCOM CSS Battle Lab, November 11, 2001.

Harman, Larry, "Objective Force White Paper: The Expeditionary Support Force (ESF) and Maneuver Sustainment Support (MSS)," Fort Lee, VA, CASCOM CSS Battle Lab, November 11, 2001.

Jeffs, Steven, "Health Service Support Planning Considerations for Military Operations in Urban Terrain," student paper, Newport, RI: Naval War College, Fall 2001.

Karasik, Theodore, "Do Russian Federation Health and Demography Matter in the Revolution in Military Affairs?" in conference proceedings *The Russian Armed Forces at the Dawn of the Millennium, 7–9 February 2000,* Michael H. Crutcher (ed.), December 2000.

Knapp, LTC Cindy Lee, and LTC Dennis M. Thompson, "CSS to the IBCT," briefing slides as they appear in *CASCOM Senior Commanders Conference, 22–23 May 2002.* Fort Lee, VA, Combined Arms Support Command.

"Load Handling System Water Tank Rack a.k.a Hippo, PM Petroleum and Water (PAWS)," *http://peocscss.tacom.army.mil/pmFP/pm_paws/systems/hippo.htm,* accessed October 18, 2002.

McLean, (Major, USA) Tracey, "Training and Doctrine Command (TRADOC) Brigade Coordination Cell," briefing, Fort Lewis, Washington, received March 28, 2002.

"Objective Force Warrior: Soldiers on Point for the Nation," brochure published by the Natick Soldier Center, Natick, MA, undated.

Peltz, Eric, John M. Halliday, and Steven L. Hartman, *Combat Service Support Transformation: Emerging Strategies for Making the Power Projection Army a Reality,* Santa Monica, CA: RAND, DB-425-A, 2003.

"Precision Airdrop Distribution Concept of Support for Future Military Operations (Draft)," draft paper, Airdrop/Aerial Delivery Directorate, U.S. Army Natick Soldier Center, provided May 14, 2002.

Price, Cecily, "US Army Medical Department Center and School Overview of Doctrine Development Process and Review of DT 8-MOUT," AMEDD Center and School, Directorate of Combat and Doctrine Development, undated.

"Protocol Additional to the Geneva Conventions of 12 August 1949, and relating to the protection of victims of international armed conflicts (Protocol I)," *http://fletcher.tufts.edu/multi/texts/BH707.txt*; accessed October 21, 2002.

"Protocol Additional to the Geneva Conventions of 12 August 1949, and relating to the Protection of Victims of Non-International Armed Conflicts (Protocol II), 8 June 1977. Part III: Wounded, sick and shipwrecked," *http://www.icrc.org/ihl.nsf/1a13044f3bbb5b8ec12563fb0066f226/edb39a930fd78699c12563cd0043a86d?OpenDocument*, accessed October 22, 2002.

Ran, LtCol, IDF, "IDF Lessons Learned Brief," briefing, Quantico, VA, June 10, 2002..

Sheehan, Kathleen M., email to Michael J. Leggierir, et al., "RE: blast overpressure monitory," June 13, 2002, forwarded to Russell W. Glenn by Sean F. Del Greco, June 14, 2002.

The Army Force Management Database, *http://www.usafmsardd.army.mil/toesummary.htm*, accessed 2002.

"The Threat from Blast Weapons," *The Bulletin For Soldiers by Soldiers,* Canadian Army Lessons Learned Centre, Vol. 7, No. 3, January 2001.

TRADOC Brigade Coordination Cell (BCC), "CSS in the IBCT," briefing presenting the analysis behind logistics estimates and describing CSS concept of support for the IBCT, 2002.

Trinidad, Clifton, "Significant Challenges in Medical Care during Urban Operations," Personal notes, undated.

"Urban Sustainability," X-File 3-35.12, Quantico, VA, Marine Corps Warfighting Laboratory (MCWL), June 25, 1999.

Wagemon, Ed, presentation given at National Ground Intelligence Center Urban Operations Conference, August 2001.

"Witness the Evil," Canadian Forces Production videotape, Ottawa, DGPA-National Defense Headquarters, Cat. # 31-0898F, undated.